Land Girl at Large

Land Girl
at Large

FRANCES WILDING

PAUL ELEK BOOKS

© 1972 Frances Wilding

Published in Great Britain by
Paul Elek Books Limited
54–8 Caledonian Road London N1 9RN

ISBN 0 236 17693 5

Made and printed by A. Wheaton & Co Exeter

TO
MY MOTHER AND FATHER
Without whom this book would never
have been written

Contents

Land Girl at Large

Prologue

It is September, 1939, and I am sixteen. My education is complete—which means, my father informs me drily, that I can start learning a thing or two. Unfortunately, I don't seem to have the right kind of brain for academic education and my mathematics never reached the standard required for me to take the School Certificate. This leads my aunt to compare me unfavourably with my more erudite cousins, although I don't know what I would have done with it if I had.

I want to write, but my family is not very interested. I am a keen amateur photographer, but they aren't very interested in this either. I was born on a Saturday, but my mother says this doesn't mean anything. She wants me to stay at home until I get married. From what I see when I look in the mirror, the chances of my ever getting married seem rather remote. On the other hand, from the time that I was about three years old, whenever I got the wishbone of the chicken, I used to wish that I could have a baby. Perhaps that is why my mother wants to keep me at home.

I am hoeing cabbages in the kitchen garden. Quill, my black cat, is sitting on the path, watching me and washing her face. Overhead is a clear blue sky, with large white clouds drifting across it. A passing acquaintance looks over the hedge, regards my earth-stained dungarees with amusement, and asks facetiously, 'What, have you joined the Women's Land Army?'

The Land Army is still only a name, bringing with it a mental picture of women feeding chickens or sitting on loads of hay, and clad in the ample skirts and petticoats considered suitable for women doing land work in the last war; so I think involuntarily, Good Lord, do I look as bad as *that*?—and I push the hair out of my eyes and reply somewhat shortly, 'No! I'm just doing a bit of work!'

When I become too hot and bored with my hoeing, I lie on my back on the grass and watch the clouds floating overhead. Quill comes and sits by my side. As I watch I wonder what else I shall see coming across the peaceful blue—and how soon. Imagination changes the clouds to bombers.

I wonder what the War, now only a few days old, will bring to my sixteen years of life. Then I get up, and go on hoeing my cabbages.

I

Wrong Number

It is September, 1941. In the last two years I have learned to type and do filing and answer the telephone in my father's office. I have had a number of articles and photographs published in gardening and nature magazines. I have also written a book and acquired a small collection of publishers' rejection slips. I would have liked to spend these two years having a proper training in journalism or photography, or even domestic science, but this didn't find favour with my family. Now the War has rather more than halved my father's income, and I have to start earning my living. I am instructed to find Something To Do.

The question is, what? I spend a day in our nearest town, six miles away, looking for work. My first step is to go to the Labour Exchange. Here I see the women's supervisor who is called, quite incredibly, Miss Facer. She is very business-like and efficient, but she seems quite sure that there is no chance of anyone under twenty-one getting a job in which they can be self-supporting, other than in a factory or the Services. I do not particularly want to be a factory hand and I feel I had enough of uniform and regimenting at school. It seems that wages are regulated by age alone, so whatever job I do I cannot earn more than a pound a week until I am nineteen, when I would get thirty shillings a week, and so on.

However, Miss Facer sends me to enquire about a clerk's job in a factory; but the man I have to see isn't in for an hour, and when I go back after lingering over a cup of coffee to fill in time, I am told that they only want a woman of over thirty; so I go sadly back to the Labour Exchange.

There they have nothing more to offer except a job in a factory, winding electric coils, and so I go reluctantly to be interviewed for this, although I am not at all interested in the prospect.

After explaining what I want to the girl in the outer office at the factory, I am told that the person I was told to ask for isn't in, but while I am waiting I can fill in a form. I am given an immense form to fill in with all possible details about myself, my parents, and my past eighteen years. When I have finished it I am shown into an inner office, and the girl from the outer office comes in to interview me.

I explain that I have been sent by Miss Facer and that I have no interest in or ability for electrical work but that Miss Facer says this doesn't matter. After checking through a long list of vacancies the girl says they all require School Certificate standard or higher, and none of them offer, for my age group, more than a pound a week. 'Of course, if you were *nineteen* . . .', she says, and at this point the telephone rings and proves to be the father of the girl who is interviewing me, and she settles down for a long conversation while I look out of the window and wonder what is the difference between a coil wound by a girl of eighteen and one of nineteen—the only answer to which seems to be, ten shillings a week. So after the girl has finished talking to her father I get up rather despondently and go back to the Labour Exchange.

Here I am told that they have nothing else at all and it is really lovely in the Services; so I go home.

My father listens to my account of all this and says, 'Nonsense!'—about what I am not quite clear; and then my mother comes in and says that my aunt says a friend of hers has a daughter who is working as a civilian in the Army Pay Corps, which is now in a town thirty miles away, and of course this is *just* the sort of job I want.

I feel I should be forgiven for being dubious about it at this stage, but of course I am not. This, obviously, is how one gets jobs. Before my mother has finished I am wondering what Labour Exchanges maintain a well-paid staff for. My mother does it much better and as she doesn't even stop to let me try to say anything there can't be any objections, so that's all settled nicely now, isn't it, dear?—and before I know where I am I have agreed to go and see my aunt's friend's daughter, who is at home on leave, this evening; and before I leave her I find I have also agreed to my aunt's friend arranging an interview for me at the Pay Corps next week.

I try to get some idea of what work I shall be called upon to do, but my aunt's friend's daughter, who is called Ida, only giggles and says vaguely, 'Oh, I do filing and things —and we go to the Canteen for tea, and it's all quite fun, you know', and I say, 'What is?' and she says, 'Oh, *you* know!'—and I don't, but I feel it won't be profitable to say so again. So I give up, and wait to see what happens next.

A week later I go for the interview arranged for me by my aunt's friend at the Pay Corps. I leave home very early in the morning to go by train to a town I have never been in before, and I make my way through a lot of little back streets until I come to the Pay Corps building, which has a soldier on sentry duty outside and looks very grim. Rather nervously I present my identity card to the sentry, and go in.

I am conducted through a long, bleak room filled with tables, and men in spectacles wearing khaki, and notices all over the walls, into a little compartment at one end. Here there are more tables, papers everywhere, and a telephone; and I am interviewed by a sergeant, who says that if I work overtime—which I will, as it's compulsory—I shall be able to earn enough to keep myself, and I had better see the Sergeant-Major.

He conducts me up a flight of stone steps, through more rooms full of tables, notices, and khaki, up more steps, through another room, and into a small office. Sitting at a table here is a short, square man with a screwed-up face

13

who looks rather like a cross-bred bulldog. He is the Sgt-Major.

By this time I am quite certain that I do *not* want to work in the Pay Corps.

The Sgt-Major says he has three vacancies and he thinks I will Do, and with overtime I will get £2 a week. I say, 'What happens if there comes a week without any overtime?' and he says cheerfully not to worry about *that*, it's compulsory for the duration anyway.

As I have to find rooms in the town before I can settle anything, I ask, Can I have time to arrange this first? The Sgt-Major says, 'Come back and see me again a week from today', and I go back through all the bleak khaki-clad rooms and down all the cold stairs, and am thankful to get outside again at last.

The next step is to find rooms. My mother has decided I must go to the YWCA hostel, and has written a pre-liminary letter of enquiry. So I go there to see.

At the YWCA, I am taken to see the Matron. To my surprise she is young and fluttery. She somehow gives me the impression that she might have been born and bred in a hostel. I am not favourably impressed.

There are no single rooms available—but I can share one, at a cost, including meals, of 25s a week. I am given a form to fill in. I take it away with me and say I will let them know. I am now quite sure that I do not want to live in a YWCA hostel *or* work in the Pay Corps.

I have to hurry for my train, and arrive home late in the evening to report the day's events. When I have finished my father looks up from his paper, nods, and turns back to it again. 'So that's all settled then', he comments cheerfully.

My mother is in bed with her hair in curlers, and says that it all sounds *so* nice and I am very clever to be able to do a job like that. I want to point out that I still do not know what work I shall have to do, but I recognize the hopelessness of this and refrain. Instead I go downstairs and complete the YWCA form and resign myself to the inevitable. No one is interested in the fact that I *do not want* to work in the Pay Corps.

A week later, I go back to the Pay Corps again. I have received instructions meanwhile that I am to see a Lieutenant Mungo.

I ask for Lt Mungo and am shown into the little office on the ground floor where I was first introduced to the Pay Corps. Lt Mungo is sitting at one of the tables. He is a thin, sandyish man going grey round the edges. He asks me more questions and then rings up the Labour Exchange. After a long conversation with them he informs me that he has told them he thinks I will be suitable, and I am to go to the Labour Exchange now to fill in a form.

I proceed to the Labour Exchange and there fill in the longest form I have so far seen. I realize that I have no idea where my father was born so I write in his present whereabouts illegibly, and no one comments. I am then told that they will take up my references and let me know in a day or two.

On my way out I see a poster on one of the walls listing the trades available in the WAAF. I see that one is photography. I feel that this, even in uniform, might at least be more interesting than fun at the Pay Corps. So I note the address of the recruiting office, and set off to find it. I do *not* want to work in the Pay Corps.

At the WAAF office I am given a warm reception. The Waaf behind the desk says Certainly, I can volunteer for photography and not be put into anything else, and she gives me an application form. I fill it in and hand it back, and she smiles sweetly at me and says they will Let Me Know. There doesn't seem to be anything else I can do about it, so I catch the next train home.

By now my family are getting rather restless over the delays. I think they feel that if they do not get rid of me now, they never will. It is impossible to convince them that there isn't any urgent demand for war-workers of my age. All that anyone wants from me is a filled-in form. But my parents are behind the times and don't see the point. If it comes to that, nor do I—but they don't see *my* point either, so that is no help. I cannot convince them that I really do *not* want to work in the Pay Corps.

Eventually I receive a letter from the Labour Exchange asking me to call. Again I set off in the early morning and when I arrive at the Labour Exchange I am told that my references have been received and are in order. I am handed three official forms, and the one I filled in, and the references in a sealed envelope, together with a card of introduction to the Pay Corps. This last item seems to me quite superfluous and I wonder how many *more* times I have to be introduced to it? I am told to take them all to the Pay Offices and hand them in at Administration. This is a new one to me, but it turns out to be Lt Mungo again.

I tell him that I have applied for a photographic job in the WAAF and am waiting to hear from them. He says that doesn't matter. I say, but not aloud, that I was afraid it wouldn't.

I am told to sit and wait outside Lt Mungo's office. After a long time a private called Bunce comes up and puts several more forms down on the table in front of me, for me to sign. The first one that I pick up begins with the words 'My attention has been drawn to Paragraph II of the Something Act, 19 . .'. Private Bunce says, 'Sign that here'. I ask what is the Act and what does it say in Paragraph II, as I have never heard of it. Private Bunce looks astonished and says, Oh, do I want to *read* it?—so I sigh and sign.

I sign several more forms. Signing forms has become such a regular routine for the last few weeks that it is not until Private Bunce collects them all up and says 'Can you start on Monday?' that I realize the brutal truth.

I have signed myself into a job in the Pay Corps.

2

My new life begins. I have arranged to live at the **YWCA.**
I leave home on Sunday afternoon, after tearful farewells
from my mother and hearty ones from my father. Why,
I wonder, does everyone love you so much when you are
going away? I do not pursue the subject however. I feel
the answer may not be complimentary.

Laden with cases, I reach the hostel at supper time. I am
shown by the Matron up to my shared room. On the way
she informs me that my room-mate, one Miss Peggy Holly,
is away for the week-end, but will be coming back later in
the evening. I am rather relieved at being able to settle in
by myself. I am also rather apprehensive as to what Miss
Holly will be like. Our room is small, bare, and totally
without character, other than the character of servants'
bedrooms in Victorian novels. I notice that there is a large
crack, caused by bombing, between the window frame and
the wall. My bed stands under this window. Later I find
that snow comes in through this crack, and I have to stuff
it up with cotton-wool. I also learn that the whole hostel
is condemned property, but the sentence has not yet been
put into effect and we go on using it meanwhile.

I unpack, and feel very depressed. I don't feel I can face
the dining-room or the common-room tonight, so I get
undressed and sit on my bed, reading and waiting for Miss
Holly. At eleven o'clock the lights are turned out, this being
the signal for everyone to go to sleep (they are turned on
again at six o'clock in the morning). There is still no sign
of Miss Holly so I get into bed.

After a long time I go to sleep, although I wake up
several times in the night and lie still listening for the sound
of someone else breathing, and peer anxiously through the
darkness at the other bed, wondering what, if anything, I
shall see on the pillow. But it remains empty. There is still
no sign of Miss Holly when the lights go on in the morning.

Shortly after the lighting-up, I am startled by a terrific

clamour from below, which sounds like a summons to a cannibal feast, but is really the getting-up gong. It fails in its purpose on this occasion however as I am so shaken by it that I have to lie still for another ten minutes to recover. Then I go down to a serve-yourself breakfast, which I am far too nervous to eat, and set off for the Pay Offices.

It is still dark and very bleak outside, and I am overtaken by stage-fright and arrive in a state of panic. I go in and report to Administration, and they tell me to wait. Then I am given more forms to sign. I am handed the various cards and papers I need to authorize my entry and clock in and out from work, and then I am taken upstairs to the Sgt-Major.

The Sgt-Major looks hard at me and barks, Am I very set on doing clerical work? As I have not yet been given any idea of what work I am required to do I stammer Not particularly, but I hadn't thought about it.

The Sgt-Major then informs me that he is going to put me on the telephone switchboard. I protest that I don't know anything about a telephonist's work and in fact I have never seen a switchboard, but the Sgt-Major says I can quite easily learn. He then goes on to tell me that there has been a Serious Leakage of Military Information recently, through, he thinks, the present switchboard telephonist. He therefore wants to put on the switchboard someone entirely strange, who knows no one in the town or in the Pay Corps, and is therefore less likely to spread any information that may be overheard in the course of the day's work. (He seems to take it for granted that switchboard telephonists do listen to calls or at any rate cannot be prevented from hearing them.) I am longing to ask him whether he thinks I *look* an isolationist type and whether he will replace me if I show any signs of having a sociable nature, but I daren't—I am much too scared. My stomach is stuck somewhere under my throat. I can't swallow, much less speak. I cannot possibly become a switchboard telephonist!

The next thing I know, I am being conducted to the switchboard room, this being the euphemistic title for a

18

small box in the middle of the building, entirely filled by a hot-water radiator (the sight of which cheers me up a little), a stool, the switchboard itself, and a large, dark young woman called Mrs Mopps, who is the present operator.

Petrified with fear, I sit down in a previously non-existent space created by Mrs Mopps moving over six inches, on a chair introduced by the Sgt-Major; and my working life begins.

Mrs Mopps may be only too efficient in imparting gossip, but greatly to my disadvantage she has no ability whatever in imparting knowledge. I sit and listen and look and try, but I remain completely in the dark. Mid-morning we go over to a crowded canteen for tea. The tea is strong and sugarless, and only just cool enough for me to sip cautiously when it is time to go back. I decide in future to miss tea.

When Mrs Mopps goes for lunch she is relieved by Private Lister, who has a crooked back and a lop-sided grin. I am also relieved by this changeover as Private Lister has some real idea of how to convey to somebody something that they do not know. What had previously seemed a hopelessly complicated muddle becomes quite a reasonable series of operations. By the time Mrs Mopps comes back I have realized the essentials of the switchboard.

It is then my lunch time and I have to return to the hostel. I share a table with a dark, bespectacled female in her late thirties, who startles me halfway through a silent meal with the remark that she cannot bear having to drink water, it is so insipid. There doesn't seem to be any answer to this, but I say I don't see how it could be improved upon. My companion glares at me and says, Possibly I *like* it?— and that concludes my social contacts for the lunch hour, which would doubtless make the Sgt-Major purr if he knew.

I return to the Pay Office to find Mrs Mopps leaning against the wall of the switchboard room groaning, and complaining of pain in her side. It appears that her appendix has recently been removed and she has had Turns like this ever since. The pain gets worse, Mrs Mopps says she wishes she could die—and I begin to feel the same, as it appears I am to be left on my own with the whole switch-board for the afternoon.

However, Mrs Mopps manages to ring Administration and report the position before collapsing completely, and there they make arrangements to send her home and Private Lister takes over. This could hardly have been better arranged from my point of view and by the end of the afternoon I have really begun to understand the workings of my future job.

At six o'clock I go back to the hostel. Here the mystery of my missing room-mate is explained, as I have only taken my coat off and am brushing my hair when Miss Holly walks in. Apparently she has alternate long and short week-ends off from her job, and Matron had overlooked the fact that this was a long week-end.

Miss Holly is small and brown-haired and dimpled, and greatly to my relief bears no resemblance to the anti-water female I met at lunch. We go down to supper together and my first day in the Pay Corps is over.

3

Two weeks pass. It is decided that I am able to cope with the switchboard single-handed. Mrs Mopps retires to some other department, and I and the switchboard are alone.

On my first morning alone I sit down in front of the thing trembling all over. I find myself fixing it with a rigid glare as if trying to hypnotize it into immobility. But it's no use—the thing I most dread happens. Plop!—down goes Number 1 flap, which means the Colonel is making a call. Oh, surely it could have been someone of lesser rank for my first call on my first day!

Nervously I pick up the receiver. 'Number please, Sir?'

(It has been impressed on me that I must say 'Sir' when answering Numbers 1, 2, and 4—one Colonel and two Majors—but it feels silly when there is no indication of anyone there.) Silence. Still more nervous, I say 'Number please, Sir?' again in a louder voice. Still no reply. I replace the receiver, but the number is still signalling a call. I think for a moment. Then I ring Central Office next door. 'Sorry to bother you . . .' (there is only a Staff-Sergeant here!) 'but do you know if the Colonel is in? His number is flashing me but there's no reply.' The Staff-Sergeant goes to find out. A minute later he is back. 'Sorry! They were dusting the Colonel's desk and left the receiver off!' I heave a sigh and relax. Of course I might have realized that Colonels never arrive first thing in the mornings!

Number 1 slides back out of sight. Number 6 starts flashing me and an outside call buzzes for attention. The thing is done. I am a switchboard telephonist!

Another week passes, and another. Slowly I learn to relax and begin to take an interest in life again, instead of sitting in screwed-up concentration, waiting for calls. It is quite a small board with eighteen extensions and only two outside lines, but this makes it more difficult when they are both engaged and there is a queue of people inside waiting to make a call. I am supposed to keep track of all these and as soon as a line is available, get the number and ring the callers back. But invariably by the time I do they have gone off to some other part of the building, and can't be found until the line is engaged again.

Hanging on the wall of my cubby-hole is a chart showing the different floors and buildings which make up the Pay Offices, and giving the names of the different departments. But even so I often find it difficult to understand what is wanted. A building called 'Grant's', snapped out to rhyme with 'ants', means nothing whatever to me, and after asking for two or three repetitions without elucidation a deadlock results—and heavy and exasperated breathing from the other end of the line. I get exasperated too, but I am not supposed to show it. Mercifully the senior officers have clear precise voices, so these difficulties do not arise with them. The Colonel in particular is most kindly, and, presumably being aware that I am an amateur suffering the job for security reasons, will explain at great length what he wants if he thinks I may not fully understand. Unreasonably no doubt, this annoys me far more than the exasperated snorts of lesser beings, as I have the impression that he regards me as a perfectly 'safe' half-wit, from whom he will put up with more or less anything in the interests of national security. So I am not so appreciative as I ought to be.

Having recovered from the first shock of immersion, so to speak, in my switchboard, I start taking an interest in the Pay Corps as a whole. My observations start at half-past eight in the mornings, when I am one of a stream of assorted and mostly uniformed humanity, making its way towards the doorway of the main building, hurrying or meandering according to the time. By this doorway stands the sentry, usually engaged in chatting to a small group of other men, who is supposed to be guarding the building. Slipping unobtrusively past this individual I proceed up the entrance stairs which lead to my department, until I am arrested by an anxious voice saying 'Oi!' This is the sentry, who having suddenly realized that he has been by-passed is standing at the foot of the stairs, regarding me with the perturbed expression of a mother hen watching her brood of ducklings entering a pond. 'Do you want to see anyone?' he asks, and I feel tempted to reply that I have already seen half the personnel and am not in the least enthusiastic about seeing any more, but think better of it and say simply, 'I work here', upon which the sentry subsides and I am allowed to proceed to my job.

My acquaintance with actual people begins and ends with my entry into the building. I then go straight to my cubby-hole and for the rest of the day I am aware of my surroundings only as a series of numbers and titles, and of my fellow-workers as disembodied names. I do learn my way about the building by this means, though I feel that my outlook on it might cause the Colonel some surprise if he knew.

Working upwards, the chart in my cubby-hole begins with the Basement, which I gather is chiefly remarkable for the Main Card Index, and for Lt Sandars who was put in charge of this floor owing, according to Mrs Mopps, to his dislike of draughts. The Basement offers variety on this point, being damp instead. In the Basement also are the Stores, dealing mainly I gather with Blue Pencils, White Papers, and Red Tape; and the laundry and the Orderly Corporal. The latter seems to have become somewhat lost, since the Orderly Room is, for some reason, in Detachment Office, also known as Central Administration—not to be confused with Central Office, which is outside my door.

From the Basement, I observe as I go to my hole, a flight of stairs leads up to the ground floor, with an open door at the top marked with white chalk 'Please keep this door shut'.

This floor is called Wing 1, and is uninteresting except for numerous pieces of cardboard hanging from the ceiling, which I first took to be left-over Christmas decorations, but later find are the numbers of the sections and are repeated on my chart, 1 to 5. These, according to my chart, deal with men whose names begin with A to those beginning with Gz, although what the latter are doing in the British Army I can never understand.

At one end of this floor is Detachment Office, where I was first interviewed, presumably so called because it is at least semi-detached, being a built-in wooden shed on its own. This is where Lt Mungo lives, also three Lance-Corporals and Private Bunce, who apparently make up Central Administration.

The next floor up is the most important floor of all, containing as it does one Colonel, one Major, one Sgt-Major, Central Office—and the switchboard telephonist.

In Central Office itself is Staff-Sergeant Baker, who maintains a more or less permanent telephonic connection with Detachment, from where I gather he was recently moved. Next door is another office containing Lt Needler and the Sgt-Major who let me in for this job in the beginning, who apparently carry on the job of interviewing applicants for employment who have passed through Detachment and survived.

Next to this is Major Bland's office, Number 2 on my board. Major Bland is known to me as an immense bass voice, with the infuriating habit of putting in a call, telling me to get the number and ring him back, and then promptly leaving his office for an unknown destination. I naturally do not realize this until I have his call waiting, and can get no reply from his office; and invariably by the time I *have* found him, the call has got impatient and rung off.

'Got my call? Good . . . Hallo! . . . Hallo!!' he booms, 'HALLO! Something wrong here! No-one there! Try again! Ring me back!'—and he slams down the receiver and bolts—or so it seems to me—to yet another part of the building.

Then there is the Colonel's office, and next to it the office of the Colonel's typist; and usually somewhere around here is the civilian messenger, Pollard, a large elderly man with steel-rimmed spectacles and a heavy moustache. Also on this floor is Wing 4, dealing with Sections 14 to 17, which according to my chart are BCP, Middle East, Gibraltar and Malta, MPP, and OCTU. All these things I am likely to be asked for in varying accents and without further explanation, and am expected to know without question what is required. The first time I was asked for 'Middle East' I looked wildly round for a suitable directory; now I know it means Extension 10 and plug in without comment.

On the next floor is the Clearing Wing, under Major Stanley, an officer whose voice and presence positively ooze charm, and what can only be described as a quite misplaced bed-side manner. He introduced himself to me by putting his head round my door and making a request for a call, so that I turned round to find a pair of very blue eyes and bristling military moustache nearly touching my face, which left me completely speechless. This section also deals with Part II orders, PMA, and E and A. Other sections are always being told that 'their Part II Orders are ready', but the meaning of this so far escapes me. E and A and PMA remain a complete mystery. No one ever asks for them, and no one I have asked can tell me what they mean.

Then there are 1483s, which I decide can't be an army age group, and must be another form; Opening and Linking; and Imprest accounts, which are only remarkable to me for the occasion when I put a caller through to another section by mistake, and heard him informed by a sarcastic unknown voice that they were *not* Imprest.

All this I absorb and consider and speculate on as I sit in isolation in my hole at my switchboard. All around me it is going on, beyond the matchboard walls and crinkly glass that imprison me, so that I cannot see out or be seen (except in one place where Pollard accidentally knocked a pane of glass out with a black-out frame, most inconsiderately causing an opening directly facing the Colonel's door). But at my finger-tips, linked by wires and within my ears' range, is all the scurry and military majesty of the Royal Army Pay Corps.

There is a plop!—and number 1 drops. 'Number please, Sir?' I am not nervous now. The Colonel wants Pollard. I locate the messenger in the Basement and ring him back, speculating on the important military secrets I may overhear, and am pledged not to divulge.

'Yes, Sir . . .'—Pollard is breathless from hurrying to the telephone. 'Yes, Sir, I'll get it right away, Sir. Two cheese sandwiches, Sir . . . and Horlicks as usual?'

The Colonel is sending to the Canteen for lunch!

4

By this time, I am getting used to living at the YWCA too. I get to know the other occupants by name and nature

—which, for me, consists largely in finding out whom to avoid.

I continue to come up, presumably, to the Sgt-Major's expectations. In fact I keep so much to myself that Peggy Holly informs me that one or two hostelites have asked her, Am I an alien? I feel that this might give the Sgt-Major food for serious thought.

The hostel has few rules, but the main one is that the doors are locked at eleven o'clock each night. Anyone wanting to stay out later must ask for permission and a key. This also has the effect of denying shelter to any genuinely stranded girl seeking it after locking-up time, since no member of the staff will answer the bell after eleven o'clock.

One evening I disgrace myself by going down in pyjamas at midnight and letting in two ATS girls who have been ringing the bell and standing in pouring rain for half-an-hour. Hearing voices and seeing the light of my candle in the hall Matron emerges, still fully dressed, and very crossly says that they cannot put anyone up at short notice. But the girls are in and cannot be turned out, so I leave them to sort it out with Matron and flee back to bed. I learn later that Matron had to make up two beds herself and now thinks very poorly of me in consequence.

One night I am awakened by a sound which at first makes me think that there is a man breaking up concrete paving under my bed. Fully awake, I realize that the noise proceeds from the top drawer of my dressing-table, where I have left two biscuits. I open the drawer very gently and two beady eyes look up at me. Then a mouse springs out and scuttles away to a hole in the skirting.

The next morning I tell Peggy, who insists that I must have dreamt it, as she doesn't believe she could have slept while a mouse ran under her bed. So the next night we both lie awake to wait for the mouse to arrive.

We lie very still listening intently, and shortly after midnight there is a faint scraping sound from below our floor. We say 'Sssshh!' to each other, and hold our breath.

The intense silence is broken by the sound of a downstairs window being pushed up.

'It's some mouse—it's opening a window!' whispers Peggy.

Silence, then scrambling sounds, and heavy footsteps. We sit up in bed quite petrified. We are being burgled!

The footsteps come upstairs. They approach along our passage. Silently we creep to the door and peer out. Two female forms disappear into a bedroom at the end of the passage. We are not being burgled after all. We have merely found out how the established residents of the YWCA habitually get into the hostel after locking-up time!

After this we settle down to sleep. I am just drifting off when I hear a familiar sound. I whisper 'Peggy!' She lifts her head cautiously. 'It's the mouse!'

Peggy listens. 'Can't hear anything!' Very gently I pull open my drawer. A faint scuffling noise, and the mouse springs out, lands on Peggy's bed, scuttles across it, jumps to the floor, and disappears down its hole.

'*Now* do you believe me?' I say triumphantly. But Peggy has disappeared under the bed-clothes. Burglars are one thing—but *mice* are a different matter altogether!

The next day I arrive at the Pay Offices to find them in a state of mild excitement. We are going to be inspected by a General!

For the first hour or so I am alert with anticipation. But nothing happens. By lunch time I am beginning to feel the effects of a disturbed night. When I come back on duty after lunch I am definitely sleepy. I forget about the General. I settle into the most comfortable position on my stool. There are very few calls coming through. My head droops . . .

I am awakened with a jerk by a violent flashing on the board. Only half awake I deal with the caller, wondering how long he has been flashing me.

I take several more calls and gradually wake up. Then a call from the Colonel provides me with the information that the General has been—and gone. An awful thought occurs to me. I do not suppose he *did* include the switch-board in his tour of inspection—but I shall never know. While the General was inspecting us I was sound asleep!

5

Uneventfully the winter passes. Snow falls, and freezes on the earth, and is joined by more snow. My room at the hostel grows colder and colder, the gas-fire at 6d an hour takes too much of my spare cash (15s a week after paying for my room and board), and the common-room fire runs out of coal. The only warm spot is my cubby-hole at the Pay Offices, and I begin to regard it almost with affection, and am glad to settle myself into it on the dark mornings, and stay there, apart from the break for lunch, until it is once more dark at night.

Normally I am relieved for my lunch hour by Private Lister. One day, however, he fails to arrive. I go on with my job, until in a lull in the calls, I realize it is past three o'clock.

I am already regarded as an eccentric because I do not make use of the tea-breaks to go to the Canteen (Pollard has developed the habit of bringing me a cup, very strong but very sweet, at the Colonel's tea-time, which is a great improvement). Now it seems that someone has decided I do not need a lunch break either. Or perhaps this is a measure for still greater security? Perhaps some really important military manoeuvres are about to take place, and I am to be shut in here, day and night, until all the vital communications have been passed?

At this stage my imagination palls before reality, and urgently I ring Detachment. 'Is Private Lister there?'

'No—try Central Office.'

I try Central Office and am rather taken aback at being

answered by the Sgt-Major. Diffidently I explain that of course it doesn't *matter*, but usually I am relieved for lunch by Private Lister, and today he hasn't turned up . . .

'D'you mean you haven't *had* any lunch?' barks the Sgt-Major, horrified.

I point out that not only have I not had any lunch, but I have been confined to the switchboard for seven consecutive hours, which is against regulations, besides being more than my constitution can be expected to stand.

The Sgt-Major rings off, promising assistance, and a few minutes later Lt Needler arrives at my cubby-hole door. Profusely apologetic, he explains that Private Lister has gone sick today, and no-one realized I was without a relief. Tomorrow Mrs Mopps will be called down from Opening and Linking (so *that's* where she went!) to take over until he comes back, but today Mrs Mopps is also away and there is no-one else in the building who can work the switchboard. Pollard will bring me in something to eat at once, but . . . and . . .

I also say 'And . . . but . . .?' and the conversation comes to a mutually embarrassed stop.

'Could you possibly,' I ask Lt Needler in desperation, 'stay here and . . . sort of keep *guard* over the switchboard . . . just for *five* minutes . . .?'

Lt Needler says Yes, that will be quite all right, and he stands to attention by the door . . .

Five minutes later I return, and soothe down six irate callers. Lt Needler departs, looking quite flustered. I drink tea and eat cheese rolls (only Colonels have sandwiches!), feeling several sizes more important.

The building is full of superior military officers—but not one of them can do *my* job!

After this life goes on as before. Recovering completely from my first nervousness, and reassured that telephonists are *expected* to listen in, so long as they don't give anything away, I get a considerable amount of entertainment over the lines. Most of the conversations that I hear are not, one would think, of the slightest use to the enemy, but they do enliven my day of four enclosing walls, snow, and YWCA.

My most terrifying job is connecting two Colonels—our own, and the one at 'Grant's'. The idea is to put them both through simultaneously, so that neither of them speaks to any lesser person than the other, but in practice this is impossible. As ours is the lesser Colonel, I can never insist on the Grant's operator putting her Colonel on the line first, so I have to get ours on and then get through as quickly as possible, before he gets impatient and rings off.

The first time I get them connected I heave a sigh of relief and feel as if I had played a really important part in military strategy. But I am greatly disillusioned when our Colonel launches into a vivid description of an operation he had just had, extracting a number of teeth—'Worse than being in the ring, old boy, didn't give me a chance to hit back!'

The most entertaining calls of all inevitably come from, and to, Major Stanley. On one occasion I hear him telling some unknown female that the buttons on his braces have just burst, and he has been forced to hold his trousers up with paper clips, which are sticking into his person whenever he leans back in his chair.

It is Major Stanley who engages three new ATS typists, and omits to mention the fact to anyone else—so when they arrive, I have to put through a furious call from Central Administration to the ATS Headquarters, asking why haven't they been informed the girls were coming and who the devil gave authority for them to come anyway? The ATS commandant says sweetly 'Your Major Stanley', and the Lance-Corporal at our end says the rest of what he is feeling *after* he has heard her replace her receiver . . .

I am lost in admiration of an unknown ATS private called Brian, who wants to do store work, but is sent to us for a clerical job. Apparently she flatly refuses to do it, and her department, in desperation, rings up the commandant at ATS Headquarters, who agrees to speak to the adamant Brian herself. After a lengthy and sarcastic tirade, interspersed with meek 'Yes, Madams' from Brian, the commandant concludes breathlessly, 'Well now, Private Brian, don't you think you are being a silly little idiot?'

'Yes, Madam,' says Brian.

'Well then, *now* will you do the clerical work?' demands the commandant.

'No, Madam!' says Brian . . .

I am asked on one occasion to get an outside number, but every time I get half-way through dialling it I am cut in on by a call on another line. On the third try a shrill female voice cries in my ear 'Hallo! Is that you? This is *me*!'

One morning I wake up with a sore throat. I set out as usual, but it gets worse. I take the first calls in a husky whisper—and then I pick up the receiver and say 'Number please!' and nothing comes.

I realize that I have got my usual winter attack of laryngitis, and for hours or days, am without the tool of my present trade—my voice.

My call in hand, hearing nothing, sensibly announces its requirements, and I put it through. Panic grows on me as I realize I am not allowed to leave the switchboard, but cannot now call anyone to notify them of the disaster. Deciding that anyway I can't stay here mute I slip out into Central Office, where I immediately run into Major Bland. Major Bland is an enormous man like a battleship and I have only met him once before. I am too nervous to try to show him by signs that I am temporarily 'non-effective', nor, by all standards of etiquette, may I pass him without saying 'Good morning, sir' which of course is just what I cannot do.

Fortunately a lesser individual, Staff-Sergeant Baker, arrives at this moment announcing that Major Bland is wanted immediately in the Colonel's office. I manage to whisper, 'Sore throat! Can't talk!' to Staff Baker, who takes in the position at once, and reports for me to the Sgt-Major.

I am rather afraid that the Sgt-Major may pounce on this predicament as an additional security measure, but apparently he regards the idea as impractical, and I am given permission to go sick at once. Shivering, I make my way back to the hostel and thankfully retire to bed.

6

It seems that life will go on for ever, a series of 'Numbers please' all day and cold feet all night. But suddenly something happens. I receive a printed notice from the WAAF recruiting office, asking me to attend for a medical examination in three days' time.

Arrived at the Pay Office, I seek out the Sgt-Major and explain to him that I had volunteered for the WAAF before I joined the Pay Corps, and that Lt Mungo said it didn't matter—and, I ask, may I have permission to attend for the medical on Friday?

The Sgt-Major looks dejected, having only just trained me and unsociable telephonists apparently being rare, and says Don't I *like* being on the switchboard? I say cheerfully, 'No, not very much', and he looks more downcast than ever. But he gives me permission to attend for my medical exam.

I set off at twelve o'clock on Friday morning for the WAAF recruiting office. Here I wait in a long line of applicants, all sitting on wooden benches and watching a door at one end of the line. We sit here until one o'clock, watching people coming and going through the door, and we grow more and more hungry and more and more apathetic.

Eventually I am called in with three others and—I might have known it—given a form to fill in. On it I am asked to state what trade I wish to volunteer for and whether I am willing to be drafted to any other. This point established, I am told that there are no photographic vacancies available at present, but I will be notified as soon as a vacancy does occur. I shall not have to have a medical examination until a job is available.

It is now three o'clock and I go out thoroughly disillusioned to get a quick lunch—at Woolworths, as everywhere else is closed between two and four o'clock.

Then I return to the Pay Offices and report to the Sgt-Major. He is immensely cheered by my report, and says Probably I'll move with them after all.

The Move has been a topic of speculative discussion for some weeks past, but my knowledge has been gleaned only vaguely from calls between our Colonel and the War Office, and more definitely from Lt Needler, who comes into my cubby-hole and quite unnecessarily chucks me under the chin and tells me we shall soon all be going West.

This does seem all too probable at this stage of the War so I do not enquire further, and I do not like being chucked under the chin anyway. But now I do say without a great deal of interest, 'Where to?' and the Sgt-Major says affably that it's a very nice place and will be lovely in the summer, and I ought to stay; so I say 'All right', and go back to my switchboard.

After this I am really curious to know more about the Move, but no information comes through my switchboard except that we should have Moved three months ago but it was cancelled when they found that the destination had leaked out prematurely through my predecessor; and we should have gone where we *are* going, last month, only the building reserved for us was requisitioned, by mistake, by some other authority.

I am much impressed by the present secrecy which appears to be watertight even from a switchboard operator, until I get a letter from my mother saying Do I know yet exactly when the Pay Corps is making its move to Bournemouth?

All this makes me think very hard about my career and

the apparently imminent possibility of my remaining permanently as a switchboard telephonist, which I do not want to do in the least; and I finally come back to my original conclusion that *I do not want to work in the Pay Corps.*

This seems to be a good opportunity to detach myself from it so I write to my mother telling her that I have had my preliminary examination for the WAAF and will be called up as a photographer shortly, and add that I have Information that the Pay Corps is moving to Leicester, not Bournemouth, and I hate the Midlands and would it be possible for me to wait at home when they move until I am called up for the WAAF?

I have only just sent this letter when Corporal Banks puts his head round the door of my cubby-hole and says Will I be moving with the Pay Corps or not?

I say this depends on where we are moving *to.*

Corporal Banks says that I must make a definite decision now as their lists have to be completed.

So I take a deep breath and say, 'No, I won't.'

After this I wait in great suspense for my mother's reply. Then I get a letter from her saying she knows it is Bournemouth the Pay Corps is moving to, not Leicester, as my aunt's friend told her that Ida said so, and surely I haven't been listening in to secret information as that would be very Wrong?

I write back and say the General himself told me it was Leicester when he made his inspection of the Pay Offices, and Lt Needler insists on chucking me under the chin while I am helpless in my cubby-hole, and I am sure I would be much safer in the WAAF.

My mother replies that she has just heard from my aunt's friend that the Pay Corps is going to Leicester next month, and Ida is not going because the air would be so bad for her chest, and she has heard that WAAF photographers go to a seaside resort in Lancashire for training, won't that be nice?

Soon after this I learn from a call by the Colonel that

the Move to Bournemouth has been postponed indefinitely as they can't find a suitable building, and the authority which has requisitioned the intended one cannot be persuaded to de-requisition it as they cannot find a suitable one either. I hope fervently that news of this does not reach Ida and my aunt's friend.

It is now nearly Spring, I have had three months in the Pay Corps, and I receive a printed letter from the WAAF stating that my application is receiving attention. On the strength of this I write to my father and tell him that I am going into the WAAF and as I have had laryngitis nearly all winter I feel I should have a few weeks' holiday first, and without waiting for an answer I give two weeks' notice to my Sgt-Major.

Several days later I get a letter from my mother saying she is so glad that I am coming home as they are preparing for their local War Weapons Week and she is getting up a concert, and I can be a great help selling tickets.

So I say Goodbye to the Pay Corps.

II

Bolt from the Blue

I arrive home to find great excitement prevailing over War Weapons, and spend several weeks going from door to door selling concert tickets, and being told that I *have* Grown, dear.

After the Week is over life settles down and in the ensuing calm my family start remembering that I am in the WAAF and asking awkward questions about it. As the weeks go by my parents show signs of increasing restlessness, and the production of my printed communications from the WAAF fails to convince my father that anything is being Done about me. So once again I set out to look for a job.

This time I start by looking at the 'Situations Vacant' column in the local paper, where I see that a local drapery store is advertising for a clerk in their wholesale department. I catch a bus into the town and apply for this. I am interviewed by one of the directors, who asks if I am any relation of my father, whom he apparently knows; and I am eventually engaged at £1 a week.

On the following Monday I leave home at eight o'clock in the morning to start work. I go as directed to the Counting House, where I shall be working, and am introduced to its other occupants—Miss Pitt, an exquisitely made-up twenty-year-old London evacuee, Miss Sellars, a small dark woman in her thirties, and Mr White, who is head of the department and my immediate boss. I spend most of the day being shown what I have to do, and am still not sure what it is at the end of it.

After a few days which I spend typing accounts and filing, Mr White tells me that I am to learn to use the book-keeping machine, which is a sort of electrically-operated typewriter that can do arithmetic. My lack of mathematical ability being only equalled by my lack of mechanical ability, I tackle this with considerable apprehension.

Mr White patiently shows me how it works and what I have to do, and then retires to his desk. I start off cautiously and for a time all goes well, but suddenly when I touch what I believe to be the right button to get the total of my column of figures, the carriage of the machine slides violently to one end and gets stuck there, jerking in and out at a terrific rate and making a noise like a machine-gun.

Mr White jumps up and runs over to it, but the carriage jabs him in the ribs every few seconds when he tries to get near it. He dodges it frantically for several minutes, telling me to press several buttons, which however only produce extraordinary noises from inside the machine.

By now several other people have come running in from other rooms to find out what the noise is, and after some time spent in giving me frantic instructions and making ineffective grabs at the thing, someone with more intelligence than the rest of us suggests that we should turn it off.

When this is done silence falls and Mr White approaches to find out what has happened. He fiddles about with it and then turns it on again, but nothing happens. Eventually he finds that a wire has broken away in the plug. He spends a considerable time repairing it, and having finally joined the ends of the two wires on to the screws after a long struggle, he proceeds to take off what he says is the old bit of wire that had broken, but which turns out to be one of the ends he has just joined on. When at last he has got it working again it is six o'clock and the day is over.

I am doubtful whether I shall ever be a really efficient wholesale drapers' clerk, though I go on trying. But when I have been working in the Counting House for nearly two months, I get up one morning to find that my mother has been taken ill in the night with gastric 'flu. As my father has to go to his office, and there is no one else at home, I have to stay at home to look after her.

My mother is in bed for several days and when she gets up again she does not feel able to do anything very energetic, so it is decided that I should give up my job and help at home for a time instead. I take over the cooking and housework and find a cooking stove less temperamental and rather more interesting than a book-keeping machine.

I am still doing this in June, when I become nineteen; and in July my age group is called to register for National Service.

Accordingly I go to the Labour Exchange where I give all possible particulars about myself, and the clerk asks Am I married? and I say 'No', and immediately afterwards Have I any children?—I suppress an impulse to say 'Yes, ten'—and the clerk writes it all down on a form. I tell her that I have already volunteered for the WAAF and am waiting to be called up, and she says she will Look Into It.

A few weeks later I receive a summons to go to the Labour Exchange again, for an interview. I am interviewed by a very large, inefficient and disgruntled woman who informs me that they can find no trace of my application to join the WAAF and I will have to do whatever I am put into, whether I like it or not. I do not like the sound of it at all, so I pay as little attention as possible, complete a second application form for the WAAF, and go home.

At the beginning of August I receive a notice to attend at the local WAAF recruiting office for my medical examination. Feeling somehow that All This has Happened Before, I set off. But this time it really does.

There are six of us for the medical exam and we are interviewed first by a round, elderly lady and a bespectacled Waaf, who tell us all that will happen to us if we join up, and ask what trades we are interested in and so on. I ask about photography and am told that there is one vacancy which has come on the monthly quota but not on the weekly, whatever that may mean.

Then we are asked for further details about ourselves

which are recorded on our enrolment forms. I point out that I have already done it all once, and would be glad if they would see that, should my first papers be found, I am not called up twice, as I only exist once; and they say they will Look Into It.

We are then despatched, with our application and enrolment forms and several other papers, to Number 2 Medical Board Room.

Here I hand my papers to a woman at a desk, tell her No, as far as I know there is no insanity in my family, and am then handed back my papers plus another, a medical form about two feet long. Armed with all these I go through into an inner room, hand them all over to another woman, and am shown into a cubicle to undress.

I am then given an orange dressing-gown to put on and shown in to the first doctor. He is elderly and kindly, and asks me, Have I ever been in a mental home or a sanatorium, how did I get on at school, what games did I play, and what are my hobbies? I tell him I haven't, and I loathed school, and I swim and play tennis, and my hobbies are walking, cycling, gardening, photography, and writing.

He then wants to know the colour of my hair, which is fair, and my eyes, which I thought were blue, but he decides are grey. He hits my knee-caps with a small mallet, and then scratches the soles of my feet with a stick; after that he looks at my teeth, and then covers up each eye separately and asks me to read a list of figures on the far side of the room; and then he covers up my ears one at a time and whispers '723' in one and '942' in the other, which I repeat after him, although I have a nearly irresistible impulse to say 'What?'

Then he measures and weighs me, and passes me on to a woman doctor.

She tells me to breathe in and out, takes my chest measurements, and then tells me to swing my arms round, which I do, nearly knocking down half her apparatus in the process. Then I lie down and she prods me, unnecessarily hard I think, and listens in to me; after which I am passed on to the third doctor.

He is elderly with a heavily-lined, humorous face, and semi-circle glasses. He asks me if I feel well, and I say I do, except that after so much prodding I feel like a bullock at a cattle market. He laughs and tells me to lie down, looks at the other doctors' reports, and says which of my hobbies is the main one? I tell him Writing and he says What do I write about? I say Mostly about animals and birds, and he says he likes birds, they have little quarrels but never a big war; and then he has finished with me, and my medical exam is over.

I get dressed and sit and wait with the five other recruits until our papers are collected and we are led back to the office. Here we wait a bit longer and eventually I am taken upstairs to see an RAF officer who asks me about my knowledge of photography, and finally says I can have the vacancy in that trade; and I go down to the office again.

After more waiting we are all talked to again by the Waaf, at considerable and it seems to me unnecessary length, and then we go back upstairs to the RAF officer. He hands us each a day's pay—1s 8d—and ration allowance —2s—and then we sign our enrolment forms, and I am told that I shall be called up in about two weeks' time, and will go first to Shropshire.

I go out feeling rather dazed and very hungry, and spend my whole day's pay and ration allowance on a much-needed lunch.

It seems I now really *am* in the WAAF!

2

A month goes by, and I begin to think my papers have got lost again. Then I receive a letter from the Air Ministry. I open it thinking 'At last!'

It says: 'Instructions have been received at this centre to draft no more photographers. You are requested to call here at your convenience during office hours to discuss the question of your being mustered to another trade.'

Very disheartened, I present myself the next day at the recruiting office. There I am greeted by a rather nice WAAF officer who takes me upstairs to see a small, dark RAF officer, neither of whom I have seen before. The RAF officer says he is very sorry about the photography, but he has rung up London to find out if photographers already enrolled are wanted, and they are not; so I will have to choose another trade. He suggests I should go as a wireless operator. I say I have no knowledge of wireless and he says That doesn't matter, all that is needed is a working knowledge of mathematics. I say that I am not on speaking terms with mathematics, but he insists that I shall be able to do what is required. I try to explain that I simply haven't the right sort of mind, and that while photography is to me a familiar room with the light on, mathematics are an unknown room in the dark.

The Waaf says that I am obviously intelligent and that is the main thing.

I have a sudden idea and ask, If it is possible for me to get a photographic job in the WRNS, would I be allowed to have my release from the WAAF to join the WRNS? The officer says he thinks I would. I say May I have a few days in which to find out if the WRNS have any photographic vacancies? and he says Yes, that will be all right.

The Waaf then takes me over to the Naval recruiting office to get details about the WRNS. The nearest WRNS recruiting office is in a coast town fifteen miles away, but at the Naval office I am told that a Wren officer comes every Tuesday to interview intending recruits here. As today is Tuesday this seems very considerately planned. The officer is due to arrive at eleven o'clock, so as it is now ten-forty-five I am shown into an ante-room to wait.

By one o'clock I am still waiting, with two girls who

came before me, and two others who have arrived since. We wait until half-past-one, by which time three other girls have joined us, one of whom has been told that the Wren officer *must* come by two o'clock owing to a medical board at two-thirty.

By two-thirty there are ten intending recruits altogether and another of them goes to the office to ask for information. She comes back and says she has been told that the Wren officer is on her way with fifteen recruits for the medical board and should arrive by the next train.

At three o'clock a civilian official from the recruiting office comes in, profuse with apologies. It appears that a Wren officer comes here from one depot on the first and third Tuesday of each month, and from another depot on each second and fourth Tuesday. Today however happens to be a *fifth* Tuesday! Consequently no arrangements have been made for a Wren officer to come from either depot, and the medical board has been called in error!

The ten of us thereupon depart in varying degrees of exasperation, having been further informed that the WRNS office in the nearest coast town is at the Royal Hotel. I call at the WAAF office and tell my officer the result of my day's exertions, and with a promise to let them know as soon as I have located a sufficiently informative Wren, I go home.

When I tell my father all this he says he has to go to the coast town the next day, so he will take me in the car.

When we arrive in the town I locate the Royal Hotel without difficulty, and I go to make enquiries. But I am informed that they cannot give me an interview here, I must go back to my local recruiting office. Thoroughly exasperated I point out that I spent four hours there yesterday waiting for a Wren officer who didn't turn up, and was told to come here by an official. Surely, I ask, *someone* here can supply me with some information about the service?

The Wren in charge says, Oh yes, they can tell me anything I want to know.

I explain that I want to volunteer for a photographic job. She says I had better write to London about that. And adds, Am I trained?

I say, No, not professionally—I wanted to take a training course. 'Oh', says the Wren, 'We only take highly skilled recruits, and we only need photographers with an *extensive* knowledge of the Continent!'

I do not ask how, after nineteen years of life, three of them War years, a girl is expected to have acquired this extensive knowledge. Nor do I draw the Wren's attention to the particulars given in their literature regarding photographers, where it states that recruits for that trade should have 'A good secondary education. Skill with hands. Professional photographic experience useful but not essential.' I merely acknowledge defeat and decide that I am not destined to become a golden-crested Wren, after all.

The next day I go back to the WAAF recruiting office, and tell them I will try to be an RDF operator after all, and risk failing in the maths.

Within a few minutes it is arranged that I shall go to Gloucester in three weeks' time, in the middle of October. It is eleven months after I made my first application—but I am really in the WAAF at last!

3

The day of my departure arrives. I pack one small case with all the things listed on my sheet of instructions, and present myself at nine o'clock in the morning at the Recruiting Office.

Here I am joined by the three other recruits who will be travelling with me. I am introduced to Irene Smith, who is put in charge of us for the journey, because she is the eldest and the only one of us who has been to London before. We are given further instructions and directions, our travelling warrants and papers are handed to Irene, and we set off.

On arrival at Liverpool Street we have to cross over to Paddington by Underground. It seems that it was some time since Irene was last in London. Or perhaps being in charge of three other people confuses her. Anyway, at Liverpool Street station she leads the way precipitately down a flight of steps, which, something tells me, do *not* lead to the underground railway. The other two follow her, but I hesitate and stay where I am. A sudden outburst of shouting from below confirms my suspicions. Irene and the others return in great embarrassment from the Gentlemen's Lavatory.

This episode shakes Irene's confidence completely. But I have been looking around me and observing notices, and I firmly lead the way to the trains. It occurs to me that I can find my way about London quite well, provided I am not rushed and can read stories on the way. So like this we arrive at Paddington.

Our train leaves Paddington at four-thirty. It is quite dark when we reach Gloucester. At the station we report to the RTO as instructed, and from there we are escorted by a uniformed Waaf through several dark corridors, and left to wait while she goes in search of a second Waaf, a corporal, who was to have met us there too. As soon as she has disappeared the corporal turns up, and then we have a further wait while the corporal goes to look for the first Waaf who had gone to look for the corporal. But at last we are led outside, where an RAF transport awaits us.

It is ten o'clock when the transport reaches its destination, and I am falling asleep. I wake up with a jerk and we all get out into a pitch-black night and a steady downpour of rain. I can neither see nor hear, nor imagine my surroundings, but I have a feeling that although this is disconcerting it may in some ways be an advantage.

We are escorted through the damp darkness by an invisible Waaf with a torch, to a long hut full of benches

45

and luggage, where we are told to leave our cases, and allowed to get out soap and towels, feel our way into an adjoining hut, and wash. Then we set out again into the night.

Again we follow the flickering torch which is our only guide to the unknown, across muddy, streaming ground, until we come to another hut. Here we collect knives, forks and spoons, one of each per person, and sign for them; then out again into the darkness and the rain to yet another hut.

Here we are told to strip to the waist, and line up for an inspection of hands, skin, and scalp. Then we dress again and set out once more, clutching our cutlery, and arrive this time at the cookhouse, where we are given a hot meal and mugs of hot tea.

Surely now we will be allowed to sleep?—but no, off we go again through rain and darkness to yet another hut. This one is actually furnished, with a carpet and easy chairs, and a desk at which an officer sits. Here we are told to sit down and wait.

I am nearly asleep when the officer tells a corporal to turn on the wireless. An invigorating military band arouses in me the first optimistic feelings I have had since we left London. 'That's fine', says the officer approvingly. After a few minutes the music fades and a guttural voice announces "Hier ist der nachricht im Englisch sprechen . . .' Two Waafs collide with each other in a frantic rush to turn it off!

Nothing more happens for some time until a cat strolls into the hut, surveys us all meditatively, and then walks over to me and jumps on to my lap. He is still there when the officer suddenly gets up to address us.

'Your time in this camp', she begins, 'will be absolute Hell . . .' and I receive a glare for murmuring 'Hear, hear!' '. . . but it is only for five days', she goes on, 'and after it is over you will start your real life in the WAAF . . .'

When she has finished a brief talk on the glory of the Women's services and the WAAF in particular, we are got on the move again, but only to the other half of the same

46

hut, where we show our identity cards, state our religions, and are given Naafi chits.

It is now midnight, and we are apparently finished with at last. We are conducted through the pouring rain to our hut, where thirty newly-arrived recruits are left, wet-through and shivering, in the care of a corporal for the night. Here there are thirty camp beds in a row down each side of the hut, and to each is allotted three dark grey blankets, two light grey sheets, and a straw-filled pillow. We make up our beds under the corporal's instructions, head and feet to the wall alternately all the way down, to conserve air.

By this time I am not only shivering, but my head aches and my throat is sore. We are told that we can lie in until half-past seven in the morning, but no-one seems able to sleep. The night passes in restless and uncomfortable wakefulness, interspersed by people getting up and lighting cigarettes or talking, and being sleepily reprimanded and hushed by the corporal. I have only just drifted into an uneasy sleep when the bugle sounds at six o'clock the next morning, and although I suppose it to be the Reveille it sounds to me more like the Last Post.

Shivering and miserable, I get up at seven-thirty, very conscious of a sore throat and a threatening cold in the head. No one seems very cheerful, as we are shown how to fold our blankets at the heads of our beds, and sweep the hut out and polish the floor. We all troop out to the cookhouse for breakfast at eight-forty-five—and have at the same time our first sight of the camp. Long, green-grey huts at all angles on all sides—long, green-grey hills in the distance and long, green-grey clouds overhead—that is Innsworth and it is not very inspiring. Nor is breakfast, and my throat is getting more and more painful. I am beginning to take what I gather is called in the Services a very dim view of the WAAF.

47

4

Immediately after breakfast we are marched to a hut called T2, for our Intelligence Tests.

First we are given a long talk by an officer on how to behave in uniform and how to do our hair under our caps, and other matters of military importance. Then we are each given three test papers, each one divided into four parts, with a time limit to complete them by.

The first is English grammar, more or less, and quite easy, although being conscious of the time limit gives me a sense of panic which cannot improve my intelligence, and I can feel my temperature going up several degrees.

The second is a matter of completing patterns which have a bit left blank, like they do in modern nursery schools; and the third is dividing a large shape into three given smaller shapes, which I do rather erratically because I am constitutionally incapable, even with a ruler, of drawing a straight line.

When at last the papers are gathered up I feel quite exhausted and rather ill, but I do not want to go sick as it would presumably mean prolonging my stay at Innsworth, so I say nothing about it.

By then it is dinner-time and after dinner we go for our trade tests. When my turn comes I am called to a table by a curly-haired officer with blue eyes, and subjected to a refined form of torture.

She gives me a very small piece of paper and draws a cross on it.

'Mark in North, South, East, and West', she says, and I do.

'Mark North-North-West . . .'

'Mark South-South-East . . .'

'South-South-West . . .' and I do all that.

'Draw a square the sides of which are one-and-a-half inches long.'

I suppress the query 'How long are the ends to be?' and

stop myself in time from saying 'Can I have a ruler?' I am no good at this sort of thing but I do my best.

'Mark off a place four-sixths of the way along one side of the square . . .'

'Now mark a place three-fifths of the way along another side . . .'

'What is four-sixths as a lower fraction?'

I say, 'Two-thirds.'

'Draw a perpendicular line from each of those marks.'

I thought a line couldn't be both horizontal and perpendicular—but the officer says most people think that.

'Draw a line two inches long . . .'

'Now bisect it.'

I have a vague idea of what this means, but am not really clear. I mark off the middle of the line.

'How would you do it with a pair of compasses?'

I say 'I don't know.' I cannot imagine why I should want to do it, with or without compasses.

The officer draws a line crossing the two-inch one. 'What angle is formed by that?'

'An acute angle—a right angle.'

'How many degrees?'

'Ninety.'

'Draw an angle of forty-five degrees.' I do.

The officer makes it into a triangle. 'What kind of a triangle is that?'

I say 'I don't know.'

'Can't you guess at it?' asks the officer.

'Yes,' I say, 'I suppose I could, but that wouldn't help you, would it?'

'It's an Isosceles triangle,' she says.

I have never heard of Isosceles before and don't know whether it is the name of a Greek philosopher or merely a geometrical term.

'Tell me the number of degrees in the other angles of the triangle', says the officer.

I look blank.

'You can work it out on paper if you like', she says.

49

'I don't know *how* to work it out', I say nervously.

The officer says she doesn't think I am trying.

I say I am sorry, but as I don't know what we are supposed to be doing I don't know how to *start* trying.

'I don't think you are as dumb as you make out', says the officer. '*Anyone* could do this test.'

'I can't help that', I say, rather stung. 'I have never possessed any mathematical knowledge, nor do I seem to have the wherewithal to assimilate it. I know nothing whatever about mathematics in any shape or form, and I told them that at the recruiting office when they sent me for this job. I am no *good* at mathematics.'

'You're not taking this seriously', says the officer, and leans back to catch a toffee thrown to her by another officer who is testing a recruit two tables away.

'I am taking it seriously', I protest. 'What do you expect me to do when I *don't* know what you're asking me?'

'A child of six could do this test', says the officer contemptuously, unwrapping her toffee.

'But I don't happen to be a child of six,' I point out. 'And if that is the case you had better get six-year-old recruits to *do* the job, because I can't'—and by then I am horrified to find tears pricking behind my eyes.

'You show no commonsense or initiative whatever', says the officer through a mouthful of toffee, and turns to another officer with very dark blue eyes and dark hair, who has just finished testing a recruit at another table. 'Says she can't do a test that a child of six could pass', she explains to the new arrival. 'Sheer nonsense, anyone with any intelligence at all could do this test.'

The new officer looks at me as if I were an insect under a microscope.

I say wearily that I am sorry, but it wasn't my idea to apply as an RDF operator at all, that I told them I have no knowledge of mathematics and I haven't, and as I shall obviously be of no use whatever in the WAAF if I have no intelligence, could I be failed in the test and take a voluntary discharge?

The second officer says firmly '*Anyone* could do this test.'

I say that this is obviously an incorrect statement, because *I can't*. And also, I add, I have a very sore throat, so could I go now?

'You should have reported sick', says the officer.

I say I don't want to report sick, I want to go home.

'You will report sick at once', says the officer. 'Do you realize you are talking to an officer of the WAAF?'

'Do *you* realize', I am stung to retort, 'that *you* are talking to a very unimpressed civilian?'

'Go outside at once and I will have you taken to the sick bay', says the officer, going rather pink in the face, 'and I will see you later when you are in a better mood.'

'A sore throat isn't a mood', I object, 'any more than ordinary intelligence has any connection with a knowledge of mathematics . . .'

But as my throat is really painful now and I have a burning headache as well as a growing desire to cry, I follow her to the door without any further protest.

Outside I am left to wait, standing in a cold wind, for my escort; and eventually a small fair Waaf turns up, and leads the way to the MI Room.

Here again I wait, until an orderly comes and takes my temperature, and says I must gargle.

I say I can't gargle—it is another of the things, with which the WAAF seems to present me in ever-increasing numbers, that I have never been able to do.

'You have been *ordered* to gargle, so you *must* gargle', says the orderly.

'I *can't* gargle', I say, 'I don't gargle, and what is more I won't gargle', and the orderly says it only requires self-control.

I say then that is another thing that I haven't got, and unless she knows how to gargle people by force, what does she propose to do about it?

The orderly says I had better have a mouth-wash.

I am then conducted back to my hut to collect my things, and from there I am taken to the sick-bay. By this time it

51

is five o'clock and I am thankful to undress and get into bed, where I immediately fall asleep.

5

I am in the sick bay for forty-eight hours with a feverish cold, and rather enjoy it. On the third morning I am told to get up and go to the MI Room to report. I wait there for over an hour and then I am shown into a small room where an officer is sitting at a desk, and she asks me how my cold is and says I can go.

So I go back to my hut and wait another hour to see the corporal in charge. When she arrives I go with her to Hut T2 and start all over again where I left off two days ago, with the two officers whose names are Hooper and Goss.

They appear to think that I shall now as a matter of course be able to do the RDF test, and are rather taken aback when I repeat my request for my discharge. I point out that I told them that before and if I have wasted the time of my King and Country in the sick bay it is their own fault. Whether I have a sore throat or not, *I have no knowledge of mathematics*, and I have at least sufficient intelligence to know that I cannot possibly do an RDF operator's job. Further I now have a firm conviction that I am not the sort of person they want in the services and I think it would be far more sensible if I were given my discharge as having failed in my trade test, rather than start up another discussion as to whether I know an Isosceles triangle when I see it or not.

They regard me with bewilderment as I explain all this and shake their heads and exchange meaning glances, but eventually they give it up and give me up too, much to my relief.

I am told to go and sit on a bench on the other side of

the room, with a small group of rejected recruits comprising a tall dark girl with Nerves, a small Welsh girl with bleached curls, a Londoner with a piercing voice and an unpleasant smell, a Scottish girl with red hair, and a large sandy Scots-woman with a grievance against everybody; also a meek-looking middle-aged woman who joined up in a hurry to spite her husband after a quarrel, and is now desperately trying to get out because she has a child of four who had been crying all night before she left.

Eventually I go before an officer who asks me to sign a form stating that I have failed as a photographer and have elected to be discharged rather than re-muster to another trade. I refuse to sign this and point out that I have never been given a test as a photographer, and she says 'Oh, but does it matter?'—and I say, To me, it does, and she looks puzzled and then makes out a fresh form saying that I have failed as an RDF operator. I sign this and am told to report to another officer at ten o'clock the next day.

After breakfast on the following morning I report to the officer, in company with the five other dischargees—the woman with the husband and child has been refused a discharge, and has to stay, in floods of tears, as a cook.

We all proceed to Hut T3, but find it locked; and when we try the next hut we are told by a Waaf inside that we have come to the wrong one. At length we reach Head-quarters and after another long wait we have our full descriptions recorded and our train warrants are given to us, and we are informed the times of our departure trains —mine leaves at twelve o'clock the next day. Then we are taken to another hut where we hand in our cutlery, and are given four days' pay. All this takes until the middle of the afternoon, and we are then free until we leave the camp.

I shake off my fellow-dischargees and go for a walk round the camp. Eventually I come to a hedge bordering one boundary, and a stile—and beyond it is a field with cows grazing in it, and willow trees.

The field is out of bounds, but then I am no longer a Waaf, and there is no-one in sight anyway. I climb over the stile and sit on the short grass. I watch the quiet cows and smell the damp evening air. The sky slowly deepens to violet and grey over my head.

I sit and think, and dream. The WAAF camp behind me, the swarms of women in uniform, the sarcastic faces of officers Goss and Hooper, all seem to fade into unreality. The earth beneath me is solid and real, the grass breathes peace and eternity, and it is refreshing to look at cows after so many blue-grey Waafs. I go on looking, and thinking, and gradually an idea forms in my mind, and hardens into a decision.

The next day I turn my back on Innsworth and travel alone to London, and home. I have been so occupied with getting in to, and getting out of, the WAAF, as well as having two days in bed, that I have not written to my parents since I left. It is ten o'clock at night when I arrive at the door, and I have some little difficulty in convincing them that I am not a ghost, and still more in explaining why I am not a Waaf.

'And now', says my father heavily, half-an-hour later, '*now* what do you suppose you are going to do with yourself?'

But I have already thought of that.

Firmly I tell him, 'I'm going on the Land.'

III

Poet's Purgatory

The idea had come to me while I watched the cows at Innsworth, and all the way back in the train I had been thinking about it. The Services, obviously, want only the mathematically-minded—or cooks. Animals and plants I do at least know something about. And monotonous though hoeing may be, I feel cabbages are infinitely preferable to perpendicular lines and isosceles triangles.

The Land Army, previously the source of a standing joke among my friends, has come into my mind on the level of a reasonable proposition. From being mildly funny, it appears intelligent and practical—a thing in which I can get down to earth without delay. I am still enthusiastic when, on the morning after my bolt from the blue, I arrive at our local Labour Exchange.

Here I am directed to Room 1, where I explain to a woman official that I have been failed as an RDF Operator in the WAAF, and have got my discharge in order to volunteer for the Land Army.

The official looks up some papers and says What a pity, recruiting for the Land Army is closed until next February.

I say Does that mean I can join in February?—and she says no, because I am now of calling-up age and must take up some form of war-work before then. But she suggests that I should go and see the secretary of the WLA to make quite sure there are no vacancies.

So, rather dashed, I set off for the WLA offices, which I find at the top of four flights of stairs, and make enquiries; but the secretary says no, they are closed for recruiting until February.

Disheartened, I return to the Labour Exchange.

Here I explain the position again to a different official, who tells me at once that if I am prepared to work in a beet sugar factory for the winter, I can go into the Land Army in the Spring. She says they are also drafting into the sugar factories land girls who have been 'stood-off' from land work for the winter. And she suggests that I should go to the nearest factory for an interview the next day.

So, slightly cheered, I return home, feeling I am at least in sight of land at last.

The next afternoon I set out for the sugar factory, which is a five-mile railway journey away from my home, and stands on the bank of the river that flows past my bedroom window.

After being asked to wait in various different places for various different people, I eventually find myself waiting for the supervisor in the factory canteen, which is empty except for myself and another girl, who is in tears.

'Are you applying for a job?' she asks as I sit down to wait. 'It's a rotten place here', and she wipes her eyes with a very damp handkerchief. I feel this is not an encouraging introduction. It appears that she has been changed from the job she was doing to another that she doesn't like, and she wants to leave; but she is not allowed to do so as she has signed on for the whole campaign, which is compulsory. I try to comfort myself by remembering that it *is* only for three months and then I can return to my cabbages, and do my best to cheer up my companion by suggesting that she may after all be transferred back to her old job before the end of the campaign.

At length the supervisor arrives and proceeds to deal with us both. After some argument my companion agrees to try the new job again and see how she gets on, and, still sniffing slightly, goes back to the factory.

Then the supervisor turns to me and says she is sorry, but she doesn't think they have any more vacancies. She goes on to say they might possibly want someone in the laboratory, but she isn't sure; and while I am wondering how to explain that I have no knowledge of chemistry she calls one of the forewomen to take me over to the factory to see.

The factory turns out to be an inferno of heat and noise, and the laboratory is situated in the middle of it. I follow the forewoman through the deafening roar and rumble of machinery in motion, through a sickening smell of beet-pulp, up a steep, slippery iron stairway, past groups of half-naked labourers covered in hair and sweat, through more noise and smells, until we come to a sort of shed built in on the first floor, which is the laboratory.

Inside the noise is only slightly less and the heat is stifling. The forewoman leads me over to a large square man with a collar and tie on and shouts that this is Mr Wasp who is in charge of the laboratory; and that I am applying for a job.

Mr Wasp says that he does need more girls in the laboratory, in fact they are very short-handed. I ask what I have to do and am shown a row of different solutions being filtered through pink filter paper, and a machine called a polarimeter where the filtered solutions are polarized and the results recorded. I look through the polarimeter and can see nothing at all. Mr Wasp asks why I use my left eye and not my right, and I explain that it is because I can only wink my right eye, which is true but sounds odd when shouted in the ear of a strange man.

I ask does it matter that I don't know anything about chemistry but Mr Wasp says No, not at all, no one does when they start but I'll soon learn. He adds kindly that Nobody is able to think clearly in this heat, the laboratory ought really not to be inside the factory at all, and people are always making mistakes because the heat affects the brain.

On this encouraging note I am engaged for the duration of the campaign. I am taken back to the supervisor's office, which seems unnaturally still and quiet after the factory, and I sign the official contract and several other forms; and then I walk back to the station and catch my train home —neither Waaf nor land girl now, but a factory hand.

2

I start work at the factory four days later. Officially I start one day before this—but that happens to be my day off.

We work in three shifts—2 pm to 10 pm, 10 pm to 6 am, and 6 am to 2pm, two weeks on each. I start working on the 2 to 10 shift. The heat in the laboratory is stupifying and all-enveloping. A girl called Joyce with dark curls on her forehead, who is the charge-hand, shows me my job. I have to test samples of waters and pulp for sugar content. The waters are filtered and polarized, the pulp dried and weighed. The results are all recorded in a large book. Samples are brought up regularly every hour : five diffusion waters in numbered cans, raw juice, diffusion pulp, and scum cake. Sweet water and diffusion juice are brought up every two hours, norit cake very occasionally, and five diffusion juices in bottles once every shift.

The waters and juices come up looking and smelling horrible, thick and cloudy and dark grey, but after I have added lead and distilled water and left them to filter, they come through quite clear. As soon as sufficient has filtered through to pour into the polarimeter, it is polarized. There is a long tube leading into the polarimeter, with a funnel at the end. Samples which give a low reading are poured into the machine through this. Samples which give a high reading are poured into a short tube with a funnel in the middle, which is then placed in the polarimeter.

Then the reading is taken by looking through the eye-piece, like a telescope, and adjusting a screw on the polarimeter until no shadow is visible on the screen. The correct reading is then showing on the scale at the top.

When I put my first sample in and look through I can

see nothing but a blur. After several attempts, I try adjusting the setting of the eye-piece itself. I find that if I screw it right back I can see perfectly clearly. I feel rather pleased at having thought of this and go back to my bench to prepare the next one.

A few minutes later Mr Wasp emerges from the polarizing room saying crossly 'What has happened to the polarimeter?'

I feel suddenly guilty and explain. Mr Wasp looks puzzled and goes back to the polarizing room with me. I look through and give him the reading of his sample. He then screws the eye-piece forward again, looks through himself, agrees that I am right, and says 'Now try'. I look through again but there is nothing but a blur.

Mr Wasp scratches his head and says have I ever had my eyes tested? I say No, except when I was passed for the WAAF. Mr Wasp looks even more puzzled and says he supposes I am long-sighted, as the normal setting is too close for me, and it can't be helped.

So I go on re-setting the polarimeter every time I use it. As this is about ten times every hour it causes considerable irritation all round, as everyone else has to put it back again before *they* can see.

No one tells me the exact purpose of what I am doing, but I get the general idea that we are supposed to make sure that there is the normal standard of sugar in the beet, and not too much going into the waste products. Each sample is supposed to be within a few degrees of the normal and I suppose that any difference would mean something important. So when I do get a sample that reads abnormally high, I go and ask Joyce what I should do about it.

Joyce says It can't be that, and comes to look for herself. Then she takes a fresh sample and puts it in, with the same result.

'Well, you can't put *that* in the book, luv', she says firmly. 'There wouldn't half be a bust-up! Put it down same as the one before, see?'

And she throws the remains of the offending sample down the drain. Bewildered, I do as instructed, wondering

59

how seriously the country's sugar supply will be affected. But I gradually learn that this is the normal procedure. Those in authority just won't accept any variation from normal in the results. There is one pulp that during my whole three months in the factory, I never succeed in getting to the correct dry-weight, and have to enter the nearest likely figure in the book each shift.

So far as I can see, the whole campaign's laboratory work could be done by one girl with a little experience and imagination, writing up the book at home.

We are allowed three separate breaks during the eight-hour shift—one of twenty-five minutes and two of ten minutes each. We get tea and supper at the Canteen during these breaks.

It seems strange, almost exhilarating, to leave the noise and heat of the factory and go out into the dark, quiet night, to walk past the still, shining river under a glittering canopy of stars, to the Canteen.

Here on my first evening I have supper of scrambled dried eggs and chips and coffee, and one of the nicest home-made jam tarts I have ever tasted—and I meditate on the oddness of life. Is this really, I think, as I walk back to the factory, the way on to the land?

Re-entering the factory is like a physical blow. Smells and noise and heat rush forward and take possession of the senses, and by the time I have regained the comparative peace of the laboratory and started on the next hour's samples, I have become part of the machinery, working a rhythmic hourly sequence, with perspiration standing on my face and the harsh music of civilization beating in my ears.

The noise has its advantages. I have never been able to sing in tune, so normally I can only sing when I am alone in the middle of a five-acre field. But here, isolated in the surrounding roar, it doesn't matter. I can sing at the top of my voice—no one will know.

So my first shift comes to an end. The last hour's results are recorded, and as we put on our coats the second shift comes on duty. I walk to the station and catch the special train, run for the factory's employees. By half-past eleven I am home, and my day's work is over.

3

So my life continues, in an ordered rhythm of thudding machines and heat and work. My first problem is working clothes—when the temperature is 75° F. in the laboratory and 30° F. outside. Skirts, anyway, are awkward and unsuitable for climbing steep staircases and walking under pipes which, being cracked in many places, drip hot juice below. I finally decide on a cotton short-sleeved shirt, cotton dungarees, thick walking shoes, and a heavy overcoat. Considering the abrupt changes of temperature we go through, even going from factory to canteen and back, it is remarkable that no one seems to suffer any ill effects. We are repeatedly being reminded to put on our coats when we go outside, but often don't. At least here no one complains of draughts!

After several weeks Mr Wasp decides to promote me to charge-hand. I leave my pulps and juices and set out with Joyce to learn how. But this involves going out into the factory on various jobs, and from this my soul revolts.

My previous contact has been confined to going to and from the laboratory, and one occasion when I had to fetch my diffusion waters myself, as the sample-carrier, a languid blue-eyed Scots girl, had got behind with it while making-up her face in the polarizing room, and I didn't find out in time before she had to go for the diffusion cake. This meant climbing up a steep flight of steps and walking along a narrow path-way between hot, sticky pipes to the tank, with hot juice dripping on me all the way and the intensified noise and smell assaulting my ears and nose, and was quite enough for me; even though I was complimented by one of the labourers who saw me descending the steps with the cans and said 'D'ye know you're the only gal in the factory what *thinks*? Ye come down them steps like a sailor, back'ards!'

The factory is a nightmare to me and the idea of spending any time in it appals me. I follow Joyce to the top floor, where she has to set an automatic graph and re-fill it with purple ink; I see where the real sugar first comes out, in yellowish, greyish lumps (and where, Joyce tells me in a whisper, we can collect a few lumps for coffee when no one is looking); I go with her to the ground floor, to the sugar packing room, where at last there is pure, powdered sugar and it clings, in a glistening whiteness, to the floor, the walls, even to the ceiling, making the place with its piled bags and the girls in coloured overalls look like a scene from a Christmas pantomime.

But over it all is the blanketing heat, the clanging and roaring that must not change or cease by day or night, the heavy sickly smells in the air, the hot drips from the overhead pipes; the floors are slimy and slippery beneath my feet, and on all sides is the monochrome brown of the ancient tanks, canvas-wrapped pipes, and machinery that cannot be replaced or properly repaired while the war lasts, because it is of German make and was installed by German engineers who returned to their own country twenty years ago.

I get back to the laboratory stunned and scared, and tell Mr Wasp that I do not want to be a charge-hand.

Mr Wasp grumbles and wants to know why.

'I can't stand being outside in the factory', I yell at him. 'It's all right in here, but outside . . .'

'Upsets you, does it?' shouts Mr Wasp. 'I suppose it is a bit grim—all the noise and heat, and the men a bit rough-looking—you might call it a poet's hell . . .'

'You might call it Dante's Inferno', I shout back. 'I saw some half-naked devils with shovels stoking the furnaces down below . . .'

Mr Wasp chuckles, and says All right, I can go back

to my old job. But, he calls me back as I turn away, he wants me to go on seeing to the automatic graph upstairs, first thing every shift. The ink is in the cupboard here . . .

'And the graph is at the top of the factory!' I shout back, appalled.

'Do you really mind?'

'No, all right—thank you!'

And I go back, gratefully, to my peaceful corner among my juices and pulps.

A few days later I come into collision with Mr Wasp again. I need a small piece of apparatus of which there is only one in the laboratory, and after a long search I approach Mr Wasp and ask if he has seen the little funnel with the tube in the middle.

Mr Wasp looks at me with a supercilious air and says Do I mean the pipette? I say I don't know, but it's a glass funnel with a tube leading out of the small end. Mr Wasp says he knows what I mean, but why don't I use its proper name? I say I didn't know it had one, and anyway if he knows what I mean can he tell me where it is? He says The pipette is in this drawer, and walks coldly away.

A few minutes later, I have finished with the pipette, and want to polarize a sample of juice. I go to the polarimeter and find Mr Wasp there, using the thing I need for my sample. He turns round when he sees me waiting and says, Do I want anything now?

I point to the thing he is using.

'Yes, please, Mr Wasp', I say with dignity. 'Now I want the *tube* with the *funnel* in the middle.'

I avoid Mr Wasp after that, but towards the end of the shift he leans over my bench and pointing at my left leg says, Do I know which of Gilbert and Sullivan's operas I remind him of?

I look down to where he is pointing and see a large dark reddish stain on my dungarees.

I say 'No, which?'—and he shouts back, 'Ruddigore!'

I smile sweetly at him and say, Doesn't he know what that stain is?

63

Mr Wasp says No.

'It's the ink off your ruddy graph', I tell him.

Then I go home.

4

I look forward to starting the night shift. At first it is difficult to get used to sleeping during the day. I catch a train home at six-thirty and get in at seven o'clock in the morning. Walking up the hill from the station I am already practically asleep. I am too tired to have breakfast when I get in, only a glass of water before getting into bed. But I am awake by mid-day and can seldom sleep after one o'clock.

I find I like working at night. The time seems to go more quickly, and the strangeness of it all turns a routine into an adventure. I set off in darkness when other people are going to bed; have my mid-day dinner, meat and gravy and vegetables and fruit tart, in the canteen at midnight; and the sky is still dark, only lightening a little at the edges, when I catch the morning train home.

Everyone gets terribly sleepy and although we try to keep ourselves awake with a constant brew of black coffee, sweetened by stolen lumps of sugar for which we take it in turns to slip out, stroll by, and lift one when no-one is looking, we do all get overcome by heat and sleepiness, and there is nearly always someone, in the intervals of their job, sitting in a corner of the polarizing room sound asleep.

I learn to sleep there in brief snatches, sitting bolt upright, without really losing consciousness of my surroundings; and this is probably just as well, since on two occasions Mr Wasp comes in and gives me instructions while I am sleeping, and I automatically acknowledge them and even register them in my brain, although I do not really wake up until after he has gone out.

On each shift one girl is employed as sample-carrier. Her job is to fetch in the different samples from different parts of the factory, for testing in the laboratory, every hour.

In theory this works, but not in practice. Our sample-carrier on the night shift is a fair, moon-faced woman of about thirty, called Mabel; with, it appears, an irresistible attraction for men.

Her samples are apt to arrive with a complete lack of continuity. She brings me two lots of diffusion waters one hour, and none the next. One hour I have no samples at all, and have to fill in the nearest likely figure from the last hour's results, as she has apparently disappeared. My next hour's diffusion waters come as usual in their numbered cans, but with the enlightening explanation, 'The numbers isn't right, luv, they've got a bit mixed like. The tin marked three is one, and two is four, and five is three, see?'

Then one night my diffusion waters are nearly an hour late, and I go to investigate myself. As I come to the steps leading to the tank I hear a crash and find Mabel lying at the foot of the steps, with diffusion waters and cans all round her. She is helped up, groaning, and taken to the forewoman for first aid, and I go back to collect the samples she has lost.

When I explain to the man in charge, a large and hairy person in blue dungarees, what befell the last lot, he grunts and says 'It's them high heels, ruddy fule', which seems to meet the situation.

The next night Mabel is away, having broken her arm, and Mrs Bean, a small dark woman in horn-rimmed glasses, takes her place. My samples arrive with almost monotonous regularity until the fifth hour, when Mrs Bean comes back half-an-hour late and breathless with indignation.

It seems that she was going past one of the air-raid shelters outside the factory when she was grabbed by a man lurking in the entrance and pulled inside, while a voice in her ear muttered, 'Late tonight ain't you, Mabel luv?'

' 'E thought I was *er*!' explodes Mrs Bean, squawking like a ruffled hen. 'I says to 'im, 'oo are yer calling Mabel? I says, Me name's Kate, and you let go of me arm! *I* don't want none of yer sauce! And then 'e lets me go and says . . .' Mrs Bean pauses and thinks better of it. 'Well, 'e lets me go and I goes to have a bit of a sit-down to get over it. The cheek!—and fancy 'im mistaking *me* for 'er!'

It is some time before Mrs Bean is calmed down sufficiently to go on fetching samples, and as nothing will induce her to go anywhere near that air-raid shelter again that night, I have to fetch those from the ground floor of the factory myself. But anyway, I now know why Mabel's samples so often failed to arrive . . .

One night shortly after this there is an air raid. At least the siren goes, and as the factory is an objective of some importance everyone assumes that it is a raid on us. After all, the Germans built the place and presumably know where it is.

Mr Wasp asks if any of us want to go down to the shelters. I think he is a little surprised by the unanimous refusal.

The warning is still on when I go down to the canteen for dinner. As I walk across from the factory I hear aeroplanes overhead. The noise of their engines fades and then there is a thud of bombs in the distance. Fires are visible in the direction of the nearest town. We are not the objective after all.

When I report this on my return to the laboratory, Mrs Bean says darkly that there's worse things than bombs. And, she adds somewhat inconsequently, them air-raid shelters are cold and damp any'ow.

So we go on working uneventfully until the end of the shift.

When I get home I find my mother in a state of great agitation because there has been a rumour that a bomb has fallen on the sugar factory. And will I be *sure* to go into the shelters *at once* if there is another alarm?

I have some difficulty in explaining tactfully that to go

to the air-raid shelters at the factory is, at the moment, to be suspected, if not in actual danger, of a fate worse than death.

5

Of the three shifts, I like the six to two—the early morning shift—the least. It means getting up at four o'clock, which is an unearthly hour, and having an alarm clock to wake me, which always brings me to consciousness in a state of unreasonable panic. After a time I find that my reaction is so automatic that I am actually out of bed, with my hand on the alarm to switch it off, *before* I wake up. One morning I get cramp in my leg while I am asleep, and do not discover it until after I have got out of bed and the leg has collapsed under me, when I wake up to find myself lying, with my leg completely numb, beside the alarm clock on the floor.

It is snowing most mornings, and still dark and starlit when I go out to catch the train. It is a horrible time to start work. Most of the girls in the factory prefer it because it leaves them the afternoon free, but leaving work at two o'clock disconcerts me as much as starting at six, and I feel disarranged for the rest of the day.

On my first early shift I feel as if I were still dreaming when I arrive. My mind simply won't accept going to work at four am. I clock in mechanically and walk across to the factory through the dark cold air. The heat and noise are overwhelming when I go in. Nothing so like a nightmare can possibly be part of real life!—not at a time when one ought to be in a soft, warm bed, anyway. I walk dazedly across the sticky, slimy floor and suddenly both my feet slip in a puddle of juice. I fall flat on my back, and so come down to earth with alarming suddenness. I am momentarily knocked out; and find myself being helped

67

up by one of the chemistry experts, a Dutchman who has very little English but is most sympathetic with what he has.

'The floors—very slippy—very slippy!' he says, shaking his head.

I agree. I reassure him that I am not really hurt, only thoroughly shaken up—not to say woken up. Then, rather sore in places, I limp up to the laboratory.

Mr Wasp says Would I like to go home?—but I say that after having got here, thank you, I would rather stay for the rest of the shift.

One morning at about breakfast time a real calamity occurs. A belt comes off one of the machines and with dramatic suddenness all the machinery stops. So do all the fans in the factory.

There are no windows in the laboratory, as it is in the very middle of the factory, so its only ventilation is by the cooled air provided by the fans. The heat increases alarmingly, and with the sudden silence of the stopped machinery I feel as if I were being stifled in a hot blanket.

Apparently this really is serious, and Mr Wasp herds us all out of the laboratory without asking our views, down to one end of the factory where there are windows open to fresh air; and here we stay until the belt is put on again, the rumble of the starting machinery grows to its customary roar, and we can return to the sweltering laboratory to resume work.

But there is very little work to do, as no samples have been produced for the last hour. While we are waiting Mr Wasp comes up and asks how I am getting on.

I say suspiciously, All right, so long as he doesn't want me to be charge-hand again.

He says it is a pity, as he would have thought I would like being in charge.

I say I would, if I was, but the factory is beyond me.

Mr Wasp says it's not as bad as it used to be. 'Before the war, the employees here were mostly ex-convicts, and a few summer seasonal workers from the coast. We never had a woman in the factory, until this war.'

I ask, 'Do you still employ the ex-convicts?' but at that moment my samples arrive and someone comes in looking for Mr Wasp, so we get back to work.

I am still thinking about this information an hour or so later, when I am alone in the laboratory. Officially this cannot happen, but as no-one keeps to their own times for canteen-breaks, and several of them like to go down together, it sometimes does.

I don't know much about the men in the factory, my contacts being limited to the now-familiar sight of gangs of labourers working, stripped to the waist, in the hotter parts of the factory, and individuals in faded dungarees who draw my samples on the few occasions when I have to go and fetch them. But now I begin to wonder. What sort of crimes were the ex-convicts in prison *for*? Do they take them after petty thefts and so on or does it extend to murderers? Most of the men I have seen *look* capable of anything . . .

My thoughts are interrupted by a noise at the laboratory door. I look up and see a bulky, bearded man, stripped to the waist and with a spanner in his hand, advancing towards me.

I have never seen any of the men from the factory in the laboratory before. A glance round confirms that I *am* entirely alone. So I look up and face my visitor enquiringly.

He comes up and wipes the sweat off his forehead with the hand holding the spanner.

'Will ye get me a couple o' asperins, please, miss?' he bellows. 'This 'eat make me 'ead ache chronic!'

The laboratory is also, I remember, the source of the factory's first aid supplies. I look in the cupboard and locate the aspirin, and give him two with a glass of water.

He takes them in one gulp.

'Ar, tha's a hot old place 'ere!' he grumbles, and disappears into the factory again.

I am left pondering on the wide scope of human frailty. The heat *is* appalling, but I had supposed that men of that size were immune from it. Ex-convicts or no, I decide that in time I could probably feel quite motherly towards them all.

Some days later I am filtering samples at my bench when I become aware of a conversation between a girl called Pam and a youngish labourer at the laboratory door. That is to say I can see a conversation taking place, not hear it, and my attention is drawn to it by what appear to be frequent glances and gestures at me.

When the man has gone Pam comes over to me and says, 'Did y'see that man I was talking to?'

I say I did.

'He's fallen for you, he has, luv! Says he dreams about you every night!'

I say the factory is enough to give anyone nightmares.

It occurs to me that the influx of numbers of women into a hitherto exclusively masculine place may be as disconcerting to the regular male workers, as the thought of the ex-convicts is to me. Never could there be so unfeminine a place as this 'poet's hell'. Yet I have watched girls making-up their faces in the polarizing room, elaborately, down to mascara and eye-shadow—as regularly as my samples arrive for testing, and as painstakingly at six o'clock in the morning as at ten o'clock at night.

I cannot contribute to this exotic femininity, although I think perhaps I do not altogether deserve the sneer of the blond, burly labourer who saw me stand aside at the foot of the steps which he was descending:

'Ought to be in the 'Ome Guard, you did, lass! Stand to attention so nicely an' all!'

I wonder, not for the first time, what I am really like, but give it up for want of information. Anyway, the winter is nearly over—and I will learn to drive a tractor in the Spring!

6

February comes at last, and we receive notice of the end of the campaign. Then I am given a date for the termination of my employment, and on one sunny morning in mid-February I am handed my cards with my last week's pay, and walk away from the factory for the last time.

And proceed along a well-worn track to the Labour Exchange.

From here I am sent to the Women's Land Army offices, where I sit for quite a long time in a waiting-room, looking at a poster showing a girl with two cart horses, which is hung in two different sizes all the way round the room.

I am growing rather tired of this poster when I am called into another room to be interviewed by two middle-aged ladies, to whom I explain about the WAAF and my lack of mathematics, and who are most enthusiastic over my desire to train for some definite job, like tractor-driving or horses or looking after stock. One of them says that I ought to have a job on my own where I am given responsibility, and before I leave they suggest that I might consider going to an agricultural college in September, and taking a three-years' course for a diploma in scientific farming.

Then I am measured for my Land Army kit and asked to provide a doctor's certificate and two references, and I complete and sign the application form, and go home.

After seeing my doctor and writing for two references, I settle down again to wait. Three weeks pass, and then one morning I receive a card asking me to call at the Labour Exchange.

Here I am informed that they have just heard from the secretary of the WLA that she has not received my medical certificate, and as she assumes, therefore, that I have not passed as fit for land work, I have been handed back to the Labour Exchange to be placed in some other work.

I nearly burst, and inform the clerk that I was examined by my doctor three weeks ago, that the certificate was signed in my presence, and that the doctor said he would post it the next day. I can only suppose that either he lost it, or it has failed to arrive through the post.

The clerk says that in that case I can make enquiries about it, and with instructions to 'expedite' the certificate I am allowed to go.

I go to the nearest telephone and ring up my doctor, only to find that he is away for a week. When I explain the position to his secretary, however, she says Yes, she remembers my certificate, and it *was* posted, with another girl's, but not until a few days ago; and she is quite willing to confirm all this to the secretary of the WLA if required.

So I set off for the Land Army office, and there see a girl who says Yes, there was some question about the medical certificate not arriving; and she goes away to find out.

After a long wait she comes back and says that they have my medical certificate now, and the reference from the sugar factory; but the other reference hasn't arrived, and unless it is received within seven days my application must be rejected.

So I go home and ring up the head-mistress of my school, who had supplied the personal reference, and learn that this also was posted, three weeks ago. However, when I make clear the present emergency she agrees to write it again, and to prevent any further difficulties I arrange to call and collect it myself. This involves an hour's bus ride, but I return late in the evening armed with the missing reference and secure in the assumption that everything is now in order.

The next morning I call again at the Land Army office and hand it to the clerk, who informs me that my papers will now be sent up to Head Office and they will let me know in due course whether my application has been accepted.

So again I settle down to wait.

A month goes by. As I have heard nothing, I decide to call at the Labour Exchange to find out if anything else has gone wrong. The Labour Exchange has heard nothing either, but they suggest that I should call at the Land Army office and enquire there.

So I go to the Land Army office, and an official I haven't seen before comes out from an inner room and gives me a worried look when I ask about the delay.

'Well, the only thing that's holding up your application now', she says, 'is that the Land Army authorities are unable to take anyone who has been in the sugar factories during the winter.'

I nearly explode.

'But surely you realize that I was only sent to the factory so that I *could* volunteer for the Land Army in the Spring?'

'I know,' she says, 'but that is the position—you see, having once worked in the sugar factory, you are now liable to be recalled there for each year's campaign, and we can't send girls out to jobs if they are going to be called away for five months out of every year.'

'You mean', I say incredulously, 'that in order to volunteer for the Land Army I have had to do something which makes it impossible for me to be accepted by the Land Army?'

'Well, yes, I am afraid that is roughly the position', she says. 'We are now trying to get a definite ruling from Headquarters, but until then we can't tell you whether you will be accepted or not.'

Staggered, I go back to the Labour Exchange.

Here I see the supervisor and put my morning's developments before her. She is as incredulous as I was, and disappears to make investigations.

On returning, she explains that the Labour Exchange appears to have received entirely opposite instructions to the WLA. 'We understood that all people who had worked in the sugar factories *must* be considered for the Land Army in the Spring. But the WLA has been told that these people are liable for recall to the factory each year and because of that should not be considered for permanent jobs', she elaborates. 'The Land Army authorities are now fighting with our authorities to get a definite ruling made.'

I say, 'Well, I hope you win,' and go home.

Another week passes, and I hear nothing more. Again I go to the Labour Exchange, but they have heard nothing either, so on the supervisor's suggestion I call again at the WLA.

Eventually the official who saw me last time emerges from inside.

'Well, we *have* got something settled at last', she says, 'and we will let you know more as soon as we can.'

'Can't you tell me *what* it is you have got settled?' I ask.

'Yes, we *can* take people from the sugar factories', she says, 'and your application will have been accepted, but we are waiting for the official confirmation to come through.'

I give a sigh of relief.

'Can you give me any idea of when I shall go to a job, or where?'

'Probably in about a week's time—but we shall be letting you know about all that.'

So I retire triumphant, and have tea at a café in the town before getting my bus home.

It has taken me six months to get into the Land Army, but I *am* in it at last!

Now things really do move. A few days later I am summoned to the Land Army office again, interviewed by the secretary, and given my badge and details of my new job.

I learn that I am to go to a farm in West Norfolk, that my employer's name is Brook, that I shall be billeted with a Mrs Burrows at a cottage in the village, and that I shall be doing general farm work . . . when suddenly the air-raid siren sounds, and everyone in the office abandons what they are doing, which includes interviewing me, and proceeds to the nearest shelter. I make my way down the four flights of stairs again, and as there seems to be nothing else to do until it is over, I go down the nearest shelter too. I sit there for an hour, growing more and more impatient with the incomplete information I have already been given, trying unsuccessfully to fill in the gaps from my imagination, and wondering how many *more* delays stand between me and the land.

At last the All Clear sounds and we all emerge into daylight again, and I go back to the Land Army Office to carry on where we left off.

I am given my Land Army clothes, which look most impressive, and a travel warrant to my job. I am told that I have to go on the following Monday, and that I must look up my trains and write to the farmer to state what time I shall arrive. Eventually I am wished good luck and, laden with articles of clothing, I descend the stairs for the last time.

When I get home I put on my new shirt and breeches and green pullover. I add my Land Army tie and socks and shoes, and pin on my badge. In the evening I go for a walk and meet a passing acquaintance who calls out, 'What, are you gardening at this time of day?'

'No!' I call back cheerfully. 'I've just joined the Women's Land Army!'

IV

The Promised Land

On the Monday morning I set off, wearing my uniform, and catch a train to the small village which is my destination. When I arrive at the station I am met on the platform by Mrs Brook, my employer's wife, a tall, youngish woman with dark, tightly-waved hair, who takes me and my luggage to my billet in the car.

Although it is now April there is a gale blowing, and the straw-stacks standing in the fields we pass are being blown all over the road, while my hair looks like straw in the wind under my Land Army hat.

My billet is a small cottage standing a little way back from the road, with a grassy patch of meadowland in between, about a quarter of a mile from the farm. Mrs Brook leaves me here with instructions to be at the farm at seven o'clock the next morning, and I am introduced to my landlady, Mrs Burrows, who shows me my room.

In my room is a large bed, a wash-stand, a table, a chest of drawers, and a chair, and a low window by the head of the bed looking out over the meadow. I unpack my things, and go down to the kitchen for tea.

The next morning I wake early, and lie listening to the birds singing until Mrs Burrows calls me at six-thirty. I dress quickly, and cautiously descend the steep, twisting stairs to the kitchen. In the kitchen I hurriedly drink the milk which Mrs Burrows has left out for me, and survey, rather dubiously, my new leather Land Army boots. They look enormous, but more business-like than the shoes I wore yesterday. I put them on and cycle down the road to the farm.

At the farm I put my bicycle in a cart-shed with the men's bicycles, and meet my employer in the yard. He is a small, thin man with receding hair and horn-rimmed glasses. He tells me to go and see Bob.

I walk across the yard to the cow-sheds, where he says I shall find him. Bob is the foreman. When I look into the shed, he is sitting by a cow, milking. He looks up at my entry. 'Morning,' he says, and buries his head in the cow again. I look on nervously. I have always been rather afraid of cows.

After a few minutes, Bob looks up again. He says, 'Come here and have a try'. Obediently I sit down on the stool, but I tremble within. Milking was not one of the jobs I applied for. I daren't tell Bob I am afraid of cows.

I take hold of the two front teats. I find that once I am in position, it is possible to forget that they are attached to a cow. I close my hands on them and pull gently, but nothing happens. I go on pressing them with alternate hands—still no result.

'She may be holding it back', Bob says. I release the teats; he grabs hold of them and sends a flood of milk into the pail. I try again. This time one small jet of milk spurts out. 'You'll get it', says Bob encouragingly. He goes out and starts on the cows in the next shed. I settle down to what seems to be a hopeless job.

Half-an-hour later Bob comes back. He looks into my pail with an expression I can't define.

'Anyway,' I say defensively, 'I've got enough for a cup of coffee . . .'

After the milking, I go horse-hoeing with Bob. The gale is over, and it's a glorious day. We start on a row in the middle of the field of beet. I lead the horse up and down the rows, and after a few failures, manage to turn him into the right row each time.

When we pause, I ask Bob 'Why do you start hoeing in the middle of the field? Why don't you begin at one end and work straight across to the other?'

He says 'It's so we finish at both ends'.

I think this over for a bit, but it doesn't enlighten me. I don't pursue the subject.

After dinner we go on horse-hoeing. My feet begin to feel sore. By three o'clock I am limping, and am glad to leave off to milk. When we have finished I hobble back to my billet, and put on a pair of sandals. After tea I go for a walk round the village, but my feet are still painful. I come back and go to bed.

The next morning I can hardly walk. There are blisters on both my heels and several toes. It is agony to walk across the bedroom in slippers.

I give the boots one glance, and then put the shoes on. My feet are encased in pain. I hobble out to the farm.

On the way I wonder if I am to go horse-hoeing again. I don't see how I can walk another step. But all is well; I have to go up to the top farm to feed the bullocks, with Charlie, instead. Herbert, who is usually in charge there, is on holiday.

The day passes slowly. Charlie is young and cheerful. He takes pity on me and does most of the work—but my feet weigh heavily on my spirits. At last it is over, and we walk back to the farm.

There is a hay-field to cross on the way. The young clover is soft underfoot, so I take my shoes off. Suddenly the sun comes out, and there are birds singing. The pain vanishes. It is a wonderful sensation. Charlie is very amused; but I walk back happily in my stockinged feet.

The next day we are weeding in the wheat. I take my shoes off, roll my stockings down and double them under the soles of my feet, and work like that. Bob, seeing my state, fetches me an old pair of his rubber boots—size ten! I try them, but they chafe the blisters on my heels, so I discard them with apologies, and for the rest of the day I work in stockings.

After this I apply to the Land Army office for rubber boots. I find that I am entitled to them only because I am milking. It seems that there are advantages in this job after all!

By the end of the first week, I am no longer afraid of cows. In the morning I go to the pasture, open the gate, and whistle. The four cows look up with an air of amused detachment. Then, very slowly, in single file, they walk through the gate. I walk behind. The sun is shining, and I find I am happy. I start to sing. The cows stop and look round in astonishment. Bob says cows like music; that's probably why they object to my singing.

They stop at the pond, and wade out into it to drink. Then on across the yard, into the cowsheds. I don't know how they know which shed is which, but they do. I tie them up as they start to feed. I wash them down, fetch the pail, put on my milking coat, and begin on Rosie.

Bob comes in and starts to milk Clover. In about twenty minutes he has finished. I am still milking. He goes into the next shed. Another twenty minutes. He comes back, and watches me in silence.

I look up despairingly. 'There doesn't seem to be any end to it', I complain. Bob grins at me.

'That's new milk you're getting now', he says. 'She's making it as fast as you're getting it out.'

I run my fingers hard down Rosie's teats. He is quite right—I had finished her some time ago. 'Then you mean I could go on all day, if I milked slowly enough?' I ask him.

'Ar', says Bob, 'I reckon you would.'

The idea is unbearable. My hands are stiff and cramped already, and there's a blister on the tip of my little finger. But none of this matters, as I realize that at last I have learned to milk. I stripped my cow!

2

Days go by. I have been milking for two weeks. My hands are no longer stiff, and I can milk two cows in an hour. I get deep froth on the milk. But there are still pit-falls to be discovered.

I bring the cows in for the morning milking. I am

thinking deeply about something quite different. I start to milk Dolly. The pail is half-full, and all is going well. Dolly finishes her feed, and moves backwards. I shout 'Stand still!' She moves further back—turns round—and walks out. Mary Ann follows her. I gaze after them in exasperation. I had forgotten to tie them up . . .

I rush out to get them back. They are already on their way back to the pasture. I have to get in front of them and drive them back to the cow-sheds. I thought they knew they came in to be milked—but apparently *they* think they only come in to be fed.

Fortunately Bob is late this morning. I get them tied up and am stripping Dolly when he comes in.

While we are milking, the farmer's son Michael, aged seven, comes in to watch. He creeps up behind Bob and grabs his cap. Bob turns round and directs a stream of milk in his direction.

'You mustn't do that!' cries Michael.

'Why not?' says Bob.

'Because', says Michael with dignity, 'I'm not allowed to *have* milk unless it's boiled!'

One morning after the milking, I am told to go with the men setting potatoes, on the twelve-acre field at the top farm. In the yard I find Short, one of the horses, being yoked into a cart, and Frank, the yardman, helping Bob and Charlie to load the cart with boxes of potatoes.

We set off for the twelve-acre field, which has already been ridged ready for setting. On the way we are joined by George, who is sixty-five and only works in fine weather, and who enlivens our walk with bits of the latest gossip.

But when we arrive at the twelve-acre we stand speechless, staring. Scattered over the whole field are the broken pieces of a large aeroplane, with two soldiers standing guard over it with fixed bayonets. One of our bombers has crashed there during the night.

George is the first to find his voice again.

'Ar!' he says in awed tones. 'I reckon it were them ridges what done that!'

The soldiers tell us that the aeroplane was a Wellington bomber, and the crew apparently baled out, leaving the machine to its own devices. It only just missed a row of greenhouses, and sliced the top off a group of willow trees by the dyke, before ploughing its way across the field that was all ready for our day's work. The tail is broken right off, the propellers have fallen in adjoining fields, and the wings and body are just a tangled mess. The red fabric flapping on the fuselage looks gruesomely like torn flesh hanging on its metal skeleton. The smaller bits all over our field look as if a party of gigantic hens had been scrapping in a huge rubbish heap.

We all stand round wondering what to do about our potatoes. The soldiers won't let us go on to the field. Eventually Bob goes back to tell Mr Brook about it.

We wait until he arrives in the car, but apparently we can still do nothing until the Air Force comes. Military officers and privates keep arriving in great numbers and army cars, but they tell us that only the Air Force can give permission for anything to be done.

After we have been waiting for some time, Short gets tired of the inactivity and starts moving off with the load of boxes on the cart. The ground is rough and he is startled by everyone shouting at him, and he slips and falls in the shafts. He goes right down, and kicks and struggles in a terrifying way, all tied up in the harness and chains.

The men have to hold his head down and cut a lot of the straps away before they can release him, and as he is kicking out with his back feet all the time it is all very difficult. While this is going on I hold Patch, the farmer's dog, who appears to think he has brought the horse down himself and has only to retrieve it. In the end Short struggles up, free of the cart, and much to my relief, unharmed.

In all this excitement no-one has noticed a large car drawing up behind us. When we look round we see two Air Force officers standing beside it, in conversation with Mr Brook. After a few minutes he comes over to us and says we are to start clearing the smaller bits of the bomber off the field.

We carry off chunks of fabric, wood, and metal. There are machine gun bullets scattered all over the field, live ones, round upon round of them, and we gather these up and give them to the military to take charge of.

After we have been about an hour doing this another large and very shiny car arrives, and a large and Very Official Person gets out, and striding up clears us all, protesting, off the field. Then he turns to Mr Brook, who is protesting even more definitely.

'Oh, is this your field?' he asks.

'I'm afraid it is,' says the farmer, rather stiffly.

'Well, I've just turned all these people off,' says the Very Official Person, indicating us. 'They do more damage than the 'plane, trampling over your land—and then you can get your men on to it . . .'

'These *are* my men', says Mr Brook, crossly.

The Very Official Person looks blank, and we all go back on the field and go on picking up bits of aeroplane.

By dinner time we have cleared up as much as we can, although the body of the 'plane still lies there, groaning and swaying in the wind, and there are two massive engines half-buried in the soft earth. I go back to my billet and give my landlady a first-hand account of the morning's work.

Several days later the rest of the wreckage is removed by the Air Force. Charlie and George go to the twelve-acre field again and start digging out the ridges flattened by the bomber. I have to help Bob turn out four young calves from their sheds, to join the ten others in the yard.

The first is a large white heifer calf. Her tactics are those of passive resistance. She plants all four feet firmly on the ground and refuses to move. Bob puts a halter on her, and I haul at the rope. Bob pushes from behind. She moves forward one step, and then taking advantage of our lessened resistance, moves four steps back. We go on pushing. It has no effect. We try rattling milk pails. She still doesn't move.

It takes us twenty minutes to lead her, inch by inch, to the gate of the yard.

Once she is safely shut inside, we return for the others. The next two Bob takes singly, holding them by ears and tail. Apart from much frisking, and several attempts to double back, which I head off, he gets them in without trouble.

The last is a little bull calf with a determined glint in his eye. I have already, ironically, named him Ferdinand. As soon as the door is opened, he dashes out of the shed. Bob grabs at him as he goes past. Ferdinand charges straight through a bed of nettles, dragging Bob with him, and heads for the wheat-field. Fortunately he gets stuck half-way through the hedge. Bob, hanging on to him from behind, shouts to me. I dive into the hedge and throw my arms round Ferdinand's neck. Together we drag him back. As soon as he is clear of the hedge, he executes a sudden out-flanking movement, shakes me off, deposits Bob full-length in the nettles, and charges back towards the shed. He misses the entrance and runs full-tilt into the door, which is swinging back. There is a crash, the door is off its hinges, and Ferdinand has disappeared.

Bob picks himself up and says things to which I feel I ought not to listen, although I entirely agree. We go in search of Ferdinand, and find him wedged between the back of the sheds and the fence. We put a halter on him, and eventually reach the yard in a series of wild rushes. The rest of the afternoon we spend repairing the shed door!

When we have finished, it's milking time. I get the cows in, and leave them while I feed the calves. I see Bob coming across the yard towards me. 'Come and look at Dolly!' he shouts. 'Didn't you see she'd blown up?'

'She—*what*?' I say, and tear down to the cow-sheds. I find Dolly much swollen on one side and breathing heavily. Bob joins me. 'She wasn't like that when I brought her in', I protest.

'It's them mangles', says Bob. 'They're going rotten. Don't give 'em any more.'

We start milking. Dolly moves restlessly. I am distinctly nervous of the possible consequences. Bob says cows have been known to burst. Fortunately the swelling begins to go down. By the time milking is over she is more or less normal again.

I turn the cows out feeling rather breathless. My arms are sun-burnt, and bleeding from my encounter with that hedge. My hair looks more than ever like a straw-stack in a high wind. Land work is not beautifying, despite all poetic allusions. But it certainly isn't monotonous either. I cycle back to my billet tired but content.

3

Weeks go by. I have been milking for a month now. I can milk three cows in an hour. My dungarees will never look clean again, and I am haunted by the smell of new milk.

It is hot, and the flies are maddening. The cows swish their tails incessantly, and lash me in the face. I rest my forehead on the cow's side—she twitches her muscles, and it feels like an earthquake in my brain.

I carry pails of milk in to the farmhouse twice a day. I feed the calves on skim milk. I carry a can of milk back to my landlady every evening. And all day long I am aware of the cows grazing peacefully in the pasture—producing yet more milk. Obviously I have a job for life.

When I was first introduced to my four cows, Mary-Ann, Dolly, Rosie, and Clover, they seemed to me to be just four ordinary, very similar animals. But I was wrong. I know now that they are four very definite personalities.

They share two cowsheds—Mary-Ann and Dolly in one, Rosie and Clover in the other. Mary-Ann is a brown cow with enormous horns. For some reason they give her an extremely benevolent look. This has no bearing on her character, however.

She is the self-appointed Head Cow. It is she who leads them up from the pasture for milking. It is she who refuses to come up half-an-hour earlier on Saturday afternoons, and simply stands watching me sarcastically from the furthest end of the pasture.

She has recently discovered the bin of beet-pulp standing in one corner of her shed. She makes a dash for it as soon as I untie her after milking. Why she never goes for it when she comes in, I don't know, except that it has no oats in it, and the pulp put out in her manger has. I make a point of rushing between her and the bin. Sometimes I get there first, and a terrific fight ensues. I throw all my weight against her neck, and taking hold of her horns, push with all my strength. It makes no impression on her at all. In the end I invariably have to pull the whole bin away from her. She then marches out, chewing a large mouthful of pulp.

I have come to the conclusion that she hates being milked. What annoys her most is having to stand back against the wall. She likes standing with her fore-quarters well across the cowshed, where she can prod Dolly with her horns when she feels annoyed. When I make her stand back, she swishes her tail in fury, and when I sit to milk her, and pinion her tail between my forehead and her side to prevent it going in my eyes, she would, I am sure, go livid, if a cow could. Her eyes bulge with outraged dignity, and she sways about and stamps her feet all the time I am milking.

Dolly is a brown and white cow with a mournful, worried expression. I do not like milking her. She won't stand still, and she moos on a sad, deep note while I milk her, as if in protest against the whole proceeding. I think she is really afraid of Mary-Ann.

I try to watch Mary-Ann while I milk Dolly, but it isn't possible to stop her unprovoked aggressions. Suddenly she steps over and gives Dolly a vicious prod in the side. This is taking a very unfair advantage, for Dolly has no horns. She jumps wildly, and kicks the bucket.

The first time this happens, being still in a state of nervousness, I also jump, and the bucket goes over. Milk pours over the floor of the cowshed. I had no idea I had milked so much. It looks much less in the bucket than on the floor.

After that I become used to it. I don't jump any longer. I grab the pail, swear at Dolly, and shout across to Mary-Ann. This doesn't have much effect either, but it relieves my feelings.

Rosie is a rather nondescript brown cow with odd habits. She has suddenly developed a taste for scrubbing brushes, rags, glass bottles, anything which stands on the ledge above her manger. She pulls them down and chews them until I intervene. The last thing she took a fancy to was a mouse-trap, which was baited with cheese but fortunately not set.

When she leaves the pond after her morning drink, she invariably looks about for something to take back with her to the meadow. She will pick up twigs, sticks, old bits of wood, anything she can lift. I think she ought to be trained to retrieve at local shoots.

Clover is dried off, being in calf, so I don't have to milk her. She is due to calve in July—according to Michael, September—according to Charlie, or November—according to Bob. It is now May, so the only thing to do is to wait. I think of taking bets on it. No one seems to know. The fact seems to weigh heavily on Clover herself. She leans her head against the manger and heaves deep sighs while I milk Rosie.

In hot weather, Clover insists on wading out into the middle of the pond when they go down to drink, and standing there, waist-deep in the water—if a cow has a waist—well, she would be waist deep if she had. She ignores all shouts and swearing from the bank. In the end I have to wade in after her. She watches me suspiciously, but doesn't move. I am sure she knows perfectly well that I can't reach her without the water going over the tops of my boots. Not until I start throwing things in her direction does she condescend to come out.

It is also astonishing how much the cows resemble human beings. Mary-Ann is obviously the loud, hearty, masculine type of woman. She reminds me of an aunt of mine. The kind that strides around in tweeds and a pull-on hat and thick stockings and heavy shoes, carrying a stick, and bullies everyone else.

Or there are times when I feel that Mary-Ann must be an out-and-out Nazi—one of the SS—a sort of Reichs-Protector of the cowshed!

Dolly is one of those plaintive, worried women who always have something to look anxious about, and if they haven't, look anxious about that. One of the nervy, neurotic kind, that becomes hysterical on the least provocation, and needs humouring.

Rosie is one of those self-effacing people who give no definite impression of character and, as in this case, are usually to be found in the company of people like Clover, who definitely suffers from temperament. It is always Rosie who stands across the cowshed in hot weather, so her tail keeps the flies off Clover's face. She doesn't seem to mind if Clover gets startled and backs into her, as she frequently does. And Clover takes all this as her undisputed right, and indulges in moods and fits of depression worthy of a prima donna.

Such are my cows. When I first saw them, I didn't think I would ever get used to them; now I feel that I know them intimately. But I can't reach the heights attained by the previous land girl, who is reputed to have 'adored' her cows. I don't think I could adore a cow.

But there's one thing they have done for me. When I go for a walk now, I boldly cross fields that I would have given a wide margin not many months ago. I can't think why I was ever afraid of cows.

4

In most stories dealing with country life, the cottagers are plump, friendly, smiling and rosy-cheeked. They talk in a slow, comforting dialect, and their cottages are warm and filled with an atmosphere of peace. My landlady and my billet are nothing like that.

Mrs Burrows is a tiny little woman with a shrill, incessant voice. When something strikes her as funny, she makes me think of a bantam hen that has just laid an egg. Otherwise she is like a house-mouse—she scuttles and squeaks.

Her hair is iron grey, drawn tightly back from a small, pale, sharp face. She has beady brown eyes which see everything that goes on, and quite a lot that doesn't; she has an inexhaustible energy, and she never stops talking. I have never yet seen her sitting down, except for meals, or heard her come to a voluntary silence. She does not merely go on talking herself—she expects constant attention on my part. She talks to me if I am reading, or writing, or listening to the wireless. It is like being out in a hail-storm—you can't get away from it. It sounds like two machine-guns firing.

She is so kind that it becomes embarrassing. She expects me to eat enormously. She says, 'I don't like to see people look thin and impoverished!' As I am ten stone and a half, this doesn't seem likely yet.

She cannot see anyone doing anything without telling them how to do it. If I make a 'phone call, she tells me how to dial. I tell her I used to work on a telephone switch-board. She says one of her nieces works at an exchange. She doesn't see the point at all.

Sometimes this really exasperates me. She insists on telling me elementary facts about birds, and I've studied wild birds all my life. I decide to confuse her by going out of her depth. 'As a matter of fact', I say, 'I'm rather a keen ornithologist myself.'

She stares at me blankly for a moment. But her reply,

if irrelevant, is crushing. 'You ought to mix more with young people!' she says.

She comes into the house with a bunch of flowers. 'Nature's wonderful, you know—wonderful!' she informs me. Her manner suggests that she is personally responsible for it.

Despite the fact that I always wake up to time, she insists on calling me at half-past-six. One morning I am aroused out of a deep sleep by her voice. I shout back drowsily, and spring out of bed, horrified to think I have overslept. I struggle into my clothes in a frantic hurry. Surely it isn't always as dark as this?—but I haven't time to think that out. I feel my way to the door.

'Frances!' calls Mrs Burrows. 'I'm sorry—it's only half-past-five!' I shout 'Thank you!' again, and get back into bed. There's a lot to be said for an efficient alarm clock!

The cottage is small, damp, draughty, and spotlessly clean. I have a room to myself at one end of the house. At least, I find I have to share it with an enormous spider, but that usually only comes out after dark. It is a horrifying object—I'd rather find Goering under the bed. It has that sort of figure.

When I mention the spider to Mrs Burrows, she remarks, 'The queer thing about spiders is that wherever you drop them, they always have a bit of silk to hang by!'

Her conversation is enlivened by words mispronounced and misused. Reading aloud an account of Hitler's movements in the daily paper, she refers to him as 'the Fuchsia' —her rendering of 'Führer'. She tells me she gives her dog 'Idolized condition powders'—meaning 'iodized'—and a chicken that was ill is not 'recuperating' but 'recruiting'.

Mary, a land girl billeted with Mrs Burrows' sister, arouses the suspicions of the village by never going out anywhere, but sitting in her room reading. Mrs Burrows says she is ' a real herman!' It was some time before I realized she meant 'hermit'.

She refers to not a colony, but a 'column' of bees, and

was passed on the road by not a dispatch rider but a 'detached rider'. She pronounces 'canopy' as 'campony' and 'camouflage' as 'flamocarge'; strawberry netting she describes as 'cotton wire-netting'.

There is a wireless in the sitting-room, but we seldom have it on except for the news. The variety programmes amuse Mrs Burrows. 'The things they say!' she comments invariably on a comedian. 'Lot of squit!' Jazz also amuses her. 'All those noises they make!' she says. 'I could stand up there and make noises as good as that myself!' I restrain myself from making the obvious comment. The wireless can at least be turned off.

She is immensely houseproud and shows me every possible corner of the cottage. She shows me everything she possesses; but this can go too far. One evening I am writing in my bedroom. She asks, 'Are you busy? Can I come in?' and enters before I can answer, with a pile of her underclothing to show me. There are several night-dresses which she has laid aside in case of severe illness or sudden death. 'I want to have everything nice if I'm taken ill suddenly!' she says. 'I don't mind what rags I wear so long as I know I've got good things put away!' This point of view doesn't appeal to me, and I tell her so.

The next evening I am in the sitting-room reading, when she comes in with a pile of her husband's underclothes. She shows me his shirts. 'These are his working ones', she explains. 'He has three thin ones too—gentleman's shirts!'

Then she shows me his winter pants. I am at a loss for a comment on these. I feel I cannot say again, 'I'm sure he looks very nice in them'. It doesn't seem suitable. I don't know what to say.

One evening a man calls to see Mr Burrows. He is out, and I hear my landlady talking and laughing at the back door. She comes back into the house looking very pleased with herself, still uttering bursts of laughter.

'Did you hear what he said to me?' she demands. I say I didn't. 'He called me a rum old bugger!' she says glee-fully. 'A rum old bugger—what do you think of that?'

I dare not tell her what I think. But I am very glad to know that someone in the village shares my own opinion.

5

It is June. I am now twenty; and my agricultural education progresses daily. There is more to learn on a farm, I find, than in any clerical job. At least a typewriter is marked in black and white. There is nothing like that about a ten-acre field—or a cow.

I didn't really want to milk when I joined the Land Army. I wanted to drive a tractor, or feed stock, or look after horses. I didn't know that I was expected to milk, until I was confronted with my first cow.

Now, except on days when everything goes wrong, I like my job. I am now in sole charge of the fifteen calves and four cows. Frank, the yardman, looks after the rest of the stock, but not these. They are 'my' cows; they are 'my' calves. I feel it is almost 'my' farm. I do not tell Mr Brook this, however. I feel that he might not appreciate it.

When I am not attending to my cows, I am sent on various land jobs. For a long time I go weeding in a field of barley. 'Weeding' consists of attacking thistles with an implement shaped like a small spade on the end of a stick, known as a 'puddle'. It is a most disheartening occupation. Days grow into weeks, the barley grows above my ankles, and the thistles grow into small trees. I am sure that after I cut them down, they get up behind me and join themselves together again. I feel it would be easier to weed out the barley.

One day it pours with rain. I shelter in the dyke until it is over. When I start again, the barley is wet, and I find that one of my boots lets in water. Fortunately it then rains again really heavily, so I am able to abandon the barley and go back to the barn. Rain becomes a welcome diversion on this job. Otherwise there is nothing but thistles, and green barley, and blue sky.

At last, when I am getting thoroughly fed up with barley, Bob tells me I needn't finish the field—they'll have to leave it. I have done about an eighth, and I am exasperated.

'What's the use of the work I *have* done?' I ask him.

'There'll be less weeds next year', says Bob.

After this I am put on to sugarbeet. First the plants are 'chopped out' with a hoe, leaving small clumps about six inches apart. Then these are singled by hand.

Singling is a back-aching job. Before long I go down on my knees, and crawl along the rows. I find I can do it much more quickly and accurately that way, and I don't leave 'double 'uns'. Bob says leaving 'double 'uns' is a bad fault. I feel rather pleased with my work.

When I leave off to milk, I find Bob waiting to speak to me in the yard. 'What d'you mean by crawling along o' them rows?' he demands indignantly. 'You don't ought to kneel when you're singling!'

'Why not?' I says cheerfully, thinking he's pulling my leg. But he isn't.

'It looks bad if anyone on the road sees you kneeling,' he says. 'People'll think we're slack if they see you doing a thing like that.'

Crestfallen, I retire to my cows. It seems that I still have a lot to learn!

Before the beet is finished, three new horses arrive at the farm. I don't have anything to do with the horses, but I see them every evening as I go back to my billet, grazing by the pond in Hawks' Meadow.

The new ones are young and restless, and it takes them a long time to settle down. They have ten acres of grass at their disposal, but they insist on leaning over the fence at one end of the farmer's garden, and eating the lupins in the flower border. Every few hours someone rushes out of the house, waving things and crying 'Shoo!' On this, the horses turn round and gallop to the far end of the meadow —but within five minutes they are back at the lupins again.

None of the other horses has this craving for lupins. There doesn't seem to be any way to stop it.

One day, while I am singling beet, I hear the sound of galloping hooves on the road. I look up and see three horses running past. At first I think they are from a neighbour's farm, and wonder whose. Suddenly I realize that they are our horses. I dash across the field to head them off, but by the time I reach the hedge they have gone past. Then I see Bob and Charlie coming up the road in pursuit. I join in. It's a welcome break in the singling!

It becomes quite an exciting chase. We follow them up the road and over fields. Eventually we manage to turn them and they head towards Hawks' Meadow again. By this time we have collected a small crowd of villagers as well. Most of them arrived too late to know what the excitement is about, but they are all eager to join in.

When the horses reach the meadow, they dash through the broken fence, and then look round at their surroundings in apparent surprise. Bob, Charlie, and I arrive, breathless. The villagers gather round and make helpful remarks. Bob and Charlie start to repair the broken fence. I go back to my singling.

Later that day, we find that the escape has had more serious consequences. There are two mares on the meadow, with three-month-old foals. One of the mares, frightened by the disturbance, jumps a barbed-wire fence into the next field, and of course her foal follows. The mare gets over safely—but the foal is caught by one hind leg on the top barbs, and cannot get free. When Bob finds him, the leg is badly torn.

The mare and foal are brought up to the pasture where my cows are. Every morning and evening, they come into the horse-yard, and I hold the foal with a rope halter while Bob dresses the wound. Frank suggests treating it with a caustic pencil. This is effective, but of course it hurts. The foal jumps violently and backs away. I rub his nose gently and hang on to the halter. It's no use—the foal is stronger than I am. Together we career all round the yard. Bob follows, with a caustic pencil in one hand and a damp rag in the other, dabbing at the leg whenever he gets within range. The mare looks on with an anxious expression.

Despite all this, the wound does heal. After several weeks, it is well enough for the mare and foal to go back with the others, on the lower meadow at the top farm. By this time, the new horses are beginning to settle down.

By this time also the singling is finished. The hay isn't fit yet. Bob tells me that I can limewash my cowsheds.

He supplies me with a bag of dry limewash, half-a-dozen assorted pails, and a small pump with a spray attached. Then he leaves me to it. I start by fetching water from the pit, and pouring some of the lime into a pail. I am nearly suffocated by the cloud of lime that arises. I wish I had thought to bring my gas-mask.

I mix the lime with water. I put the end of the pump in the pail, and direct the spray at one wall. I start to pump. A trickle of pale wash runs out of the spray. I pump harder. A transparent liquid hits the wall, leaving it slightly damp.

I mix more limewash. I try again. One jet spurts out at the wall. Then nothing happens. The nozzle is blocked.

I go and look for Bob. He has disappeared. I find Frank, and he comes back with me to look at it. He takes the pump to pieces. He puts it together again. He starts to pump The spray plays over the wall.

Frank goes out. I start off again. I pump twice, and the spray becomes blocked. Infuriated, I go in search of Frank.

Frank comes back, grumbling. He clears the nozzle again. Then he pumps while I hold the spray. It keeps clear for a few minutes—then blocks up again. Frank swears, and I suggest using a brush instead.

By the end of the morning, the walls are thinly covered in watery whiteness, and the floor is flooded with thick limewash. There are patches of limewash all over my face and hair. Frank laughs every time he looks at me. We move on to the second shed.

Before we have finished it, we run out of limewash. Frank

becomes exasperated. He takes an old scrubbing brush and finishes the walls by hand, with the wash from the floor.

'I told you a brush would be more effective!' I tell him cheerfully. Frank only grunts.

I start to clean up the floors. I throw pail after pail of water over them. There seems to be limewash on everything but the walls.

I have just finished when Bob comes back. He holds out a spray nozzle, and grins broadly. 'I meant to give you this this morning', he says. 'You've been using the wrong one!'

I glare at him. This time, even I am beyond words.

6

Haysel is upon us. When I have finished my milking and feeding, I help with the hay.

The weather is stormy. I spend the morning turning hay, cut the day before. In the afternoon another storm comes up, and it pours with rain. All my work is wasted. I feel I want to go out and hold an umbrella over it.

The next day is fine, and Bob says the hay is dry enough to cart. I lead the carts from the field to the stack-yard. There's quite a long way to go, across a field of beet and down a long lane. I ride back with the empty carts.

I learn that the horses respond to particular words of command. Coop! means turn left. Wheesh! means turn right, and to reverse you call Whoaback!

I get to know the horses by name and nature. Toby, bright brown with white flecks, is powerful and fast. Broom and Smart, two dark brown mares, plod on all ~~him. Broom and Smart, two dark brown mares, plod on all~~ the time steadily and placidly. Short, golden brown, is stubborn and has ideas of his own. I ride Short through the yard, going back to the field. He gets as far as the stable door, and promptly stops. Nothing will make him move on. I have to get down from his back and lead him past.

I like Toby best. It's a wonderful feeling when he strides over the field. The cart rocks and bounces, and I sit on his back and would sing for joy, if I didn't think it might annoy him as much as it does the cows.

There is a sharp turn through the gate of the field. The first time I go through it, I nearly take the gate post with me. I only just manage to back Toby in time. After that I learn to measure the distance better. Before long we career through without difficulty.

We work until sun-down, when the field lies empty. There are storm clouds lying on the horizon. Bob says, 'It's a rotten crop.' But it's been a wonderful day.

The next morning it is still fine. We start to cock another field. After the milking, I go horse-raking.

When I arrive at the field, I ask Charlie for directions. I've never been on a horse-rake before. Charlie says, 'The rake's over there—Bert'll set you in', and he goes off.

I go over to the horse-rake—and Bert. Bert is a lad of about fourteen. I look at the rake, and Bert looks at me. No one does anything about it. I decide I'd better make a move, so I climb up, and sit on the seat. It feels very precarious. I look to Bert for further instructions.

Bert hands me up the reins. He shows me the lever that works the rake. 'Go up there', he says, pointing up the field. Then he walks away.

Feeling very nervous, I start off. I feel clumsy and awkward. I forget that wherever I go, I am raking, and get hopelessly entangled with already raked heaps of hay. I am stuck up in the middle of the field, with a horse I'm not sure how to handle and a rake that performs extra-ordinary evolutions behind me. I press the lever when I don't intend to and forget to when I ought to do it. Every time the rake kicks up, I jump. I feel an awful fool.

I arrive at the top of the field. There I find where I am supposed to rake. Cautiously I set off.

I get on all right except when I have to turn. All the men are working at this end of the field. Everyone seems to be looking at me.

When I pass Frank he shouts something, and Broom decides it might have been 'Whoa!' and stops anyway in case. Charlie shouts, 'Get on, you old bitch!' 'Me, or the horse?' I ask. We get on.

Coming back, Frank shouts to me again. I still can't hear what he says, so I stop to find out. I find that he said 'Make her keep going!'

I pass Bob at the end of the next row. 'Am I doing all right?' I ask him despairingly. 'Yes, you're doing fine', he says. This encourages me tremendously. I am suddenly aware of the warm scent of the hay, and the song of a lark overhead.

Bob wants me to change to the other rake. His wife is using it, but it's larger, and she can't reach the lever. I can.

This time I am driving Toby. We get on much better. Before long I am dashing up and down, wondering why I ever thought it was difficult.

We work late. At night I ride back on Toby. The weather is still fine, and there's a glowing red sunset.

The next day we cart the field. I ask Bob what I am to do. 'You can take that fork and go on the stack', he says.

I climb up on to the stack. There are three men on it as well. The hay comes flying up; I get nearly smothered in it. I heave great forks-full across the stack, and still more comes. I struggle with enormous lumps of it. I feel I am drowning in hay.

I get a hay-seed in one eye. A pile of hay descends on top of me when I'm not looking, and I nearly get buried before Charlie hauls me out. Frank throws hay at me from a passing cart when I lie down to rest between loads. It is all great fun. I am sorry when I have to go back to milk.

The next day we go on carting hay, and I go loading carts with Frank. I stand on the cart, and he forks the hay up to me. It's much more difficult to load right than one would imagine. The hay has to be piled round the outside first, or it won't balance. Frank laughs at my first effort. Anyway it does stay on when we take it back.

'Looks like a little house!' shouts Charlie from the stack.

'One that's been badly blasted', I acknowledge sadly. Blasted is the right word. The men find it so very awkward to unload!

We set out again. This time the load shapes better. I lie full-length on it while Frank leads the cart between cocks. I cope with forks-full of hay that seem likely to land on top of me. The load grows steadily higher.

Says Frank, 'I don't think you're really interested in this job—not wrapped up in it, like!' He throws up a lump of hay which nearly eclipses me. Through a mouthful of hay, I retort, 'Wrapped up in it! I'm so wrapped up in it I don't think I'll ever be able to get off the cart!'

By the end of the day I can load fairly respectably. I slide off the last cart as the sun goes down. The field is done.

In my bedroom I strip, and hay falls all over the floor. I brush my hair, and hay showers out of it too. I am more than wrapped up in it. I am positively impregnated with hay.

I lean out of the window before getting into bed. There's a storm coming up again, but it doesn't matter now. Our haysel is over. Let it rain!

7

When I first took charge of my cows, I seemed to be confronted with a dozen jobs all at once, and couldn't think what to do first. Now I have settled into a steady routine —although the day doesn't always go 'according to plan'.

As soon as I arrive at the farm, I get on with the milking. While I milk there are various diversions. Bob comes in to see how I am getting on. Then Frank comes in to have a look at me.

One morning Frank brings news. The old sow has given birth to twelve pigs. 'D'you want to see 'em?' Of course I do. I leave the milking and go with him to the pig-house.

There they are—twelve tiny, pink-silk-coated creatures as unlike the big clumsy sow as anything could be. Or perhaps she only seems clumsy. Anyway she is a very devoted mother.

Frank asks me to help him turn them out, to the pen he has got ready in the yard. We drive the sow out first—but the piglets are another matter. They run in all directions.

Frank solves the difficulty by taking a large broom, and using it to push the piglets gently in the right direction. They squeal loudly and fall over each other as Frank sweeps them along. I watch to see that they don't try to run back. It's the first time I've seen anyone brushing out pigs!

A few weeks later, Frank comes to the cowshed one morning with news of a different kind.

'You know that there trap', he says, 'that I set for them rats that were getting the ducks? I'll have to do something else about 'em. So far I've caught two ducks, two hens and a cat!'

'Badly?' I ask.

Frank grins. 'They'll have chicken for dinner at the house tomorrow', he says, 'but the rat took most of the ducks. The cat's only hurt in its front paw—that in't broke. That'll mend.'

He leaves me to the milking. As I milk Rosie, I wonder if the rat came out in time to see the ducks go into the trap. I feel in some ways it is a pity that rats probably have no sense of humour.

Milking over, I turn the cows out. As I pass the pond, I see a large chicken being chased by a moorhen half its size. The chicken eventually flees to the safety of the hen-house, and the moorhen returns triumphant to her natural element.

I go up to the meal-house, and get food ready for the calves in the yard—sugar beet pulp and crushed oats. I carry the food in, and the fifteen calves rush up to me. There is deep straw underfoot. I find it difficult to walk across. Calves push and jostle me on all sides.

When I have filled their mangers, I pump up their water.

Not only water comes up, for the pump leads to a pond, and there are small fish in it as well. I don't know what the calves do about these.

When the water trough is full, I get them in several forks-full of hay. The calves love this, and rush up as I bring it in, so a lot of it falls over their heads instead of in the rack. Soon all that is visible is a row of hind legs and tails. Occasionally one calf gets pushed out of line, and walks down the row until he can insert his nose between two others. There is a steady sound of rustling as they eat.

Having finished the calves, I go back to the cowsheds. I clean them out, and put beet pulp and oats in the mangers for the evening meal. After that I return to the meal-house, and mix up the calves' next meal as well. I find that I need more pulp and oats, so I go to fetch it.

The oats are in a pile in the mill-house. I fill a sack several times, and empty it on to a pile on the meal-house floor.

The pulp is more difficult. This is stored in immense bags in an old piggery. I take a barrow and wheel it between the piles of bags.

I select one which looks in the right position. I climb up on top of the pile, get behind the bag, and push. It is too heavy for me to lift.

I give a final heave, and the bag falls with a crash into the barrow. Luckily it doesn't burst. This does happen quite frequently, and I have to clear it up before I can get on. With an effort, I shift the bag into a better position on the barrow, and wheel it out to the meal-house.

Getting it off is a worse problem. I wheel it up to the big wooden bin, and heave the bag up on end. For a moment it sways on the balance; then it goes over, half into the bin. I open the top and scoop pulp out with my hands. When I have lightened it a bit, I can lift the rest of the bag over the edge.

I haul out the empty sack, and shovel the pulp over to its allotted half of the bin. I bring in two pails of water and pour over it—pulp must be damped before being used as feed. I stand upright and wipe the sweat off my face. Then I go back for another bag.

This one I take down to the cow-sheds. I carry a sack of oats down there too. By that time there is very little morning left.

Bob has told me for some time that he wants the iron-house cleared up. Every time I look at it I decide there is something else I ought to do. Bob becomes impatient. So at last I make a start.

It is a terrible job. I don't think it can have been cleared out for years. The bench is loaded with iron plough-fittings of every description. I haven't the least idea what to do with any of them. I decide that if I put everything now on top, underneath, and everything now underneath, in full view, Bob will realize that I have done something to it, anyway.

Suddenly a wild squealing makes me look up. It is coming from the pig-house. I go to investigate.

There I find Frank, bathing the young pigs in skim milk. He has a brush in one hand, and a pail of milk between his legs. In the other hand he holds a struggling piglet by the hind feet, while he brushes the dirt off its back. He goes through the whole litter systematically. The piglets scream frantically and the old sow positively roars. I have never heard anything like it in my life. It sounds as if a mass execution was taking place.

When it is over, and the last piglet has fled to its mother, a comparative silence falls. I say to Frank, 'What on earth are you doing?'

'Giving 'em a bit of a clean up', he says. 'They get dirty rolling in the muck in that there pen.'

I return to the iron-house. The ways of a farm are still beyond me.

After dinner I get on with my clearing-up again. By milking time I have finished the iron-house. It looks better at any rate. I don't know if anyone will ever be able to find anything in it now, but I can't help that. At least there is room for the men to sit and have lunch.

I get the cows in, and milk. I feed the calves again, and put the cows' morning meal in their mangers. While I am doing this I hear more frenzied screaming coming from the pig-house. It sounds desperate, so I go to investigate once again.

This time, I find all the piglets peacefully feeding at their mother's side. All but one, that is. He is standing on top of the others, squealing because they are in the way, and he can't get at a teat.

I think he is a little ashamed of himself. Anyway, he stops when he sees me standing there. After a few minutes he pushes his way in, and settles down to feed.

I watch them in silence. The ways of animals take a lot of understanding too.

I go back to my cow-sheds, and finish putting out the food. I collect the milk for my landlady. It is five o'clock. A day is over.

8

It is July. Bob decides that Clover should still give milk, as the calf isn't due yet. Accordingly he starts to milk her again. Against all rules and regulations, after standing dry for five weeks, she immediately yields a pail-full of milk.

The next day her calf is born. The date is a surprise to everyone but Clover. Bob is distinctly annoyed about it.

The calf is introduced to milk in a bucket, and removed to another shed. I am instructed to milk Clover.

Bob comes in to watch. Somewhat apprehensive, I sit down and take hold. Clover obviously resents my approach. She lifts one back leg sharply, and scrapes off my hand with an aggressive hoof. I draw back quickly, and she moves away. I follow her. She moves again. Bob leans against the wall and smokes. Clover looks round at me and glares.

I move her over to the end of her rope, and take hold again. Being unable to move further in that direction, she moves back. I am of course in the way, but this doesn't worry her. The stool overturns and I land painfully on the floor. The pail goes over with a crash. Fortunately there's no milk in it yet. Clover backs up against the wall and trembles violently.

I pick myself up and look at Bob. Bob laughs. 'She's all right', he says, lighting a cigarette. 'She's got a very sensitive skin.'

Sucking my bleeding knuckle, I say So have I.

I move her over and sit down again. She kicks out, taking another bit of skin off my hand. I draw back. 'This is hopeless!' I say to Bob.

He only grins. 'She'll get used to you', he says, 'in time.'

She does not get used to me. Instead she gets worse. She won't let me come near her. I decide to re-name her Winnie—because to me she represents blood, toil, tears and sweat. I go to Bob in despair. 'I shan't have any hands left if this goes on!' I tell him. 'They say, you know,' says Bob, 'that a cow will never hurt a woman.'

'In that case,' I say crossly, 'she is obviously entirely taken in by my Land Army breeches!'

By now everyone on the farm knows that I am fighting a battle with Clover. Every milking time they come to watch. Occasionally they make suggestions. No one offers to help. It is most exasperating.

Bob suggests putting a rope round her hind legs. This makes matters worse. She kicks and struggles violently, over-balances, and falls down. I am afraid of her breaking a leg.

Frank suggests tying a rope round her body. This is supposed to prevent her lifting her hind legs. I have no idea why. Anyway, it doesn't come off. What it does do is to turn the cowshed into a good imitation of the Wild West, and Frank into an elderly kind of cow-boy. Clover pins him against the manger, dances round the shed, and behaves like a wild thing until the rope is removed.

She is rapidly reducing me to a nervous wreck. I go on strike. Bob milks her for a few days, to give us both a chance to calm down. When he milks her she is perfectly quiet. When I milk her in his presence she only moves about a bit. When I am alone with her she knows it. She turns round and looks at me with an expression of malevolence. I don't know why she should feel like that.

Bob says it will soothe her if I talk to her while I milk. But when I am confronted with Clover, I don't seem able to concentrate on conversation. And anyhow, I can't think of anything to say. I try reciting poetry. The result is something like this:

'Abou Ben Adhem, may his tribe—Stand still!—increase —awoke one night from a deep dream—Blast you!—of peace—and saw, within the moonlight in his room— Steady!—making it rich, and like a lily in bloom—Stand still!—an angel, writing in a book of gold—Stand *still!* —exceeding peace had made Ben Adhem—Get over!— bold, and to the presence in his room he said—Keep your foot down, damn you!—what writest thou?—*Stand still!*'—

And so on. I don't know what Clover thinks about it.

This goes on for some time. Every day I enter the cow-shed prepared for battle. Every day I emerge sore and breathless with the milk. I dream about Clover. I dream that I go into the cowshed and find a tigress tied up in her place. I am expected to milk it instead. My only feeling is one of intense relief. I had no idea a cow could become so prominent in my life. I think in terms of Clover.

I give half of Clover's milk to her calf, a tiny little thing with enormous eyes. She has obviously inherited her mother's temperament. When I clean out her shed she pursues me round it, butting at me. None of the other calves does it. I look at her over the top of the door. 'I don't hold with this interfering with Nature', I tell her. 'You ought to be doing my job!'

Then one day Bob greets me with glorious news. He is

getting two young calves to put on to Clover, so I shan't have to milk her any more!

The calves arrive—little, woolly, shaky, long-legged things. Clover eyes them with suspicion. One—the brown one—starts to feed at once. Clover sniffs it over, and decides to adopt it. From then on she hates being separated from it. She moos to it when I bring her in, and refuses to leave it and go back with the others to the pasture. Obviously I was a very poor substitute.

The other calf—the black one—doesn't seem fond of milk. It doesn't even seem to know what milk is. It sniffs at Clover doubtfully and turns away. For several days it refuses to feed from her—Bob has to give it milk on his fingers. Even then it isn't very enthusiastic. When at last it does take Clover's milk, it feeds with the air of one performing an unpleasant but necessary function. I point this out to Bob. He says, 'You always do get some queer ones, even with animals'. I don't quite know how to take this. But I do feel a tremendous sympathy with the black calf.

Clover still gives me a malevolent look whenever she sees me. I am so glad not to have to milk her that I don't care; I feel quite kindly disposed towards her now. It is obviously the ideal ending to a battle. We both think we have won.

9

Harvest has come at last. As soon as I can leave my cows, I go to the harvest field.

We need all hands for the harvest—even old Herbert, who is 80, and usually spends all his time looking after the bullocks at the top farm. Herbert is obviously an isolationist. Normally he never comes into the farmyard at all. This is the first time I have seen him working in a field with the other men. Even then he works apart from them, doing a separate job.

He is cutting round the edge of the oat-field, so that the tractor and binder can get by. I help him to tie up the loose corn into sheaves.

At first we work in silence. I can't think of anything to say. Apparently the same thing troubles Herbert. After about an hour he lifts his head and says, 'Did 'ee know that there other girl that were here?' I say No, I didn't.

'Ar', says Herbert. He stands up slowly and scratches his head. 'She were all right', he says at length. 'Proper good girl, she were. Only, y'know, she didn't like me to call her dearie.' He looks at me in bewilderment. 'An' bless her', he chuckles, 'I didn't mean nothing by it!'

After that we get on better with both the work and the conversation. I find Herbert is more interesting to talk to than most of the men. Possibly being alone so much gives him more time for meditation. We discuss a wide variety of subjects, from religion to oats.

Some of the words he uses puzzle me. I cannot make out what he means when he says our soldiers will be 'fussy' about their victories. It is some time before I realize that the word means 'pleased'.

After a few days with Herbert, I find I am learning a Norfolk vocabulary. 'Chittering' means talking, 'clawing' means walking in a hurry. 'Mowlds' are small clods of earth, and 'kelter' means rubbish or a tangle of weeds on the land. A 'footpad' is a foot-path, 'feeting' means foot-marks, and a 'hangercher' is a handkerchief. To be 'a bit old' means to be a bit cunning or artful. Not that Herbert tells me any of these things; he takes them for granted, and I gradually get the hang of what he is talking about.

When Herbert and I have cut round the edge of the field, Bob brings in the tractor and binder. I am looking forward to this, as I have never seen one working at close quarters before.

I arrive in the middle of the morning, to find the field looking oddly deserted. Then I see a group of men at the far end, gathered round the binder. Apparently something has gone wrong with it.

I go over to them, and watch interestedly. It looks a most complicated piece of apparatus. At last Bob crawls out from underneath. He starts up the tractor and they get going again.

I have to clear the sheaves off the corners of the field, so the tractor can turn. It isn't a strenuous job. I have plenty of time to watch the binder.

Half-an-hour later, something goes wrong again. Once more Bob crawls underneath, and issues muffled instructions from the depths of the machinery. Again I am an interested spectator.

The third time it happens, I am less interested than I was. It is cold standing about in the field.

The tenth time it happens, I am frankly bored. I feel I know all that is necessary about binders. I go back and milk my cows.

It is late evening when we finish the field. I ride standing on the tractor as Bob cuts the last square. It is a glorious moment. The wind sings in my ears. The men stand round with guns ready, waiting for any rabbits that may be hiding in the corn. Much to my relief and their annoyance, nothing appears, except a large black and white cat.

The next field to be cut is three acres of wheat. It is so badly battered by wind and rain that the binder will not take it, and breaks down on every, instead of every other, round. Bob swears, and crawls about under the machinery, and gets tied up in binder twine, and pulls out handfuls of corn stalks—and then a dozen yards further on the thing breaks down again. Frank has to cut some very bad patches by hand, with a reap-hook. It takes the whole day to get those three acres done.

A week later, the cutting is finished. The next day we begin to cart.

I lead the carts from the field to the stack. In the intervals between carts, Bob tells me to go on the horse-elevator. I find this means walking round and round behind the horse, with the object of encouraging him to keep going. The horse is Boxer, black with a white face—the one that Herbert uses up at the top farm. Boxer, like Herbert, is old and slow. When I am behind him, he ambles round, and stops every few minutes. If one of the men appears with a stick, he puts on a sudden burst of speed—but it doesn't last. Every time he stops, he gives me a most indescribable look over his shoulder.

We work until dusk every evening. One day it pours with rain. We throw covers over the stack, and huddle under the elevator waiting for it to stop. The elevator leaks rain down the backs of our necks.

It doesn't stop. In the end we have to abandon the wheat, and go muck-carting. We cart muck at intervals all through the harvest.

One morning, as the wheat is too damp to cart, we go burning out dykes. I discover a wasps' nest in the bank of one dyke, and hastily effect a strategic withdrawal. Later on, I light by mistake a dyke which is considered too near the stacks to be fired with safety. I don't realize what I have done until I become aware of a sudden panic among the men. Bob and Frank tear across the field towards me. Fortunately we are able to get it out, and there is no damage done. I had no idea that farming could be so hard on the nerves!

So that Frank can spend all his time in the harvest field, I get in food for the rabbits, which are ordinarily his responsibility. There is a second crop of clover on the smaller hay-field. I take a reap-hook and a sack, and cut as much as I can carry.

Picking up a large bunch, I take hold of a bumble bee as well. The bee promptly stings me on the hand. I scrape out the stink with the blade of the reap-hook. My hand feels rather stiff for a time, but doesn't swell at all. I decide I must be immune from bee stings.

Coming back with my load, I see Jack, the tractor-driver, with the tractor and cultivator on an already cleared cornfield. 'When are you going to let me drive her?' I call to him.

'You can try now, if you like!' he calls back.

I drop the bag of clover and go over to the tractor. I climb into the seat. Jack shows me how to start the thing. Slowly the tractor moves forward.

I hang on to the wheel and try to steer a straight course across the stubble. Perched up on the seat, I feel most triumphant. This is really what I joined the Land Army for.

At the end of the field I stop, and wait for Jack who is following behind. 'You'll soon learn!' he says. 'You've done better than Bert anyway—he put her into the ditch!'

I look at the bit I have cultivated as I walk back. In places it looks a little like an advertisement for permanent waving. I think I will stick to my cows after all. I put the clover in the rabbit shed, and settle down to milk.

At last harvest is over. I lead in the last cart; and watch it elevated to the stack as the sun goes down.

Herbert calls to me across the field. When we discuss religion, Herbert always refers to Christ as 'The Master'. I am therefore rather taken aback when I hear him shout, 'The Master wants to see you to-night!' However, I realize that he only means the farmer, and it's nothing more important than working out my overtime.

I ride back to the farm on Boxer. A thunderstorm blows up before we get in. It begins to rain; lightning tears at the sky, and there's a crack of thunder overhead. Boxer breaks into a trot, nearly throwing me off. I grab at the halter wildly, and luckily his speed doesn't last. He is still nervous though, and gets as close as he can under a wet and prickly hedge. Branches get caught in my hair and I am nearly torn from his back. The rain pours down.

By the time we arrive at the farmyard, my hair is on my shoulders, and one of the straps of my dungarees has fallen down. And Mr Brook is waiting to speak to me. But it doesn't matter—the harvest is safely in.

It is raining only slightly as I leave the farm. A rainbow curves across the sky above the farm house.

I think of Herbert. I go clawing along the footpad to my billet, and despite being wet and dishevelled, I do feel that fussy with life!

I O

On Sunday evening, when I have finished milking, I accompany my landlady to church. We walk down the road, up the 'pightle' which is a narrow path over a field, across a meadow occupied by two goats with two white kids, and through the graveyard.

The church is a tiny building, with one bell, which is tolled funereally for every service. The congregation is so small that no one dares to sing out loud, except the Rector. Any deviation from the tune would be too obvious if they did.

I sit in a pew with Mrs Burrows and her sister, Mrs Cross, one on each side. Mrs Cross is a little woman with round blue eyes and curly white hair. Neither of them comes up to my shoulder. When we walk down the aisle together, I feel like a battleship in convoy.

The Rector is a chubby little man, with a habit of saying 'What' absent-mindedly at the end of each sentence. Mrs Burrows likes him. 'He can preach a good sermon and he can swear!' she says. This appears to be the whole village's idea of a good parson.

The lessons are read by an elderly man with imposing side-whiskers. Possibly these make his reading a little indistinct. Anyway, I am rather startled when he reads what sounds like '. . . and they made booze, and there were great rejoicings . . .' Only after he has repeated this several times, do I realize the word is 'booths'. . . .

The service is short, and it is still light when we come out. We walk back with Mrs Cross to her house. Here I am introduced to Mary, the land girl billeted with her, to whom Mrs Burrows refers as 'a herman'.

She turns out to be an Irish girl with dark, untidy hair, spectacles, and a pronounced brogue. We talk cows for some time—she is milking too—and although Mrs Burrows talks incessantly also, it's a change from just Mrs Burrows.

All the same, I am rather glad when at last we leave. Mrs Burrows goes straight back home. I go for a walk.

Further down the road is the Post Office, run by an elderly couple called Rix. Mr Rix has a bald head and a tiny tuft of white beard on the extreme end of his chin. He is postman and postmaster as well.

Mrs Rix is a greying, plaintive woman. She is as great a talker as my landlady, only in a different way. Mrs Burrows talks excitedly in jerks. Mrs Rix talks in a steady drone. Like most people, she seems to think that because I am a land girl, I must have come from a town. No one will believe that a land girl comes from the country. Mrs Rix is always saying how dull I must find it here. I don't find it dull, but she won't believe that either. Perhaps she is prejudiced. She tells me she has lived in this village for forty years, and still doesn't like the place.

Past the Post Office is The Shop. Before the War, it is reputed to have actually sold things. Now it only serves teas to lorry drivers.

On the day of my arrival, I went into the shop to get some writing paper. The girl behind the counter looked blank—they hadn't anything like that. One of the lorry drivers, drinking tea, came to my rescue. 'If you want to write something, you can have this', he said. He handed me an old cigarette packet.

Beyond the shop is The Lane. It leads, along a twisting course, to the next village.

Leaning over a gate in the lane is George. As well as doing odd work on our farm, George has his own small-holding. He lives alone in a dilapidated cottage, and looks as if he never washes. He is untidily be-whiskered—except on Sundays, when he shaves—and weather-worn.

He looks with suspicion on the aeroplanes that pass continually overhead. 'I wouldn't want to be a pilot', he says. 'I wouldn't have the cheek to drop them bombs!'

He tells me of a soldier who, given a lift by a woman driver, shot her when he left the car. 'Y'know', says George seriously, 'that there were a rare ungrateful thing to do.'

112

George is always seeing 'parachutists' drop on the village.

'There were a 'plane last night' he tells me. 'Buzzing round and round, it were—round and round—and I see something drop—' he pauses dramatically—'and it hoong', he states impressively. 'It hoong!'

He removes his pipe and points over a cornfield. 'Over there, he come down', he says. 'Two o' the Home Guard chased him through that there corn!'

I happen to know that the mysterious object was a piece of meteorological apparatus dropped by a British aeroplane —it fell on our farm, and was retrieved by Bob the next morning—but I say nothing, except 'Ar!' which is a very useful and non-committal form of reply.

I turn and walk back, leaving George by the gate, puffing at his short black pipe and watching the sky for other possible invaders.

By the time I reach the cottage it is growing dusk. Mrs Burrows has lighted the lamp in the sitting-room, and it throws a clear circle of light round the table. We have supper —bread and cheese and milk—and I go up to my room.

'Be careful of the black-out on your front window!' Mrs Burrows calls after me. The front windows are our danger points—the air-raid warden lives in the house opposite. The back windows don't matter nearly so much.

I blow out my candle and get into bed quickly, before my spider comes out. It's a feather bed and luxuriously comfortable.

Outside my window, there's a faint mist lying over the earth. The sky above is violet, edged with gold. The village lies still, wrapt in darkness, silence, and peace.

I I

Autumn has come. There is a mist over the fields when I go out in the mornings. I have to use a candle at both ends of the day.

We are getting up the potatoes. Bob drives the tractor with the spinner. The potatoes fly out behind, and the men pick them up at an incredible speed. I lead the carts from the field to the grave. One morning I take the carts to the wrong field by mistake. The men, waiting in the other field to get a load of straw, are fuming at having to stand about in a bitter east wind. When I do arrive, Bob greets me with, 'Where the heck have you been? Don't you know there's a War on?' I say bitterly, '*No*—when did it start?'—and feel like a dog that's retrieved the wrong bird.

We start work at last. I lead Broom up the field with a full cart. Short is waiting by the grave with an empty one. Suddenly our young bullocks charge across the adjoining meadow. Short is startled. He rears up, snorts, and bolts down the field. I pull Broom out of the way as he goes past. Then I dash off in pursuit of Short. I make a grab at his bridle, tread on a large potato, and fall flat on the muddy headland. Short tears on until Bob stops him at the other end of the field.

I am glad when we leave off for dinner. I help Frank to unyoke Toby from a loaded cart, 'stood down' on supports. When he is half unyoked, Toby apparently thinks suddenly of dinner, and bolts. The harness catches on the cart chains, and the belt of the saddle breaks. Toby dashes across the yard to the stable.

I look at Frank. I hand him my end of the broken harness. 'You tell Bob', I implore him. Then I also bolt. I carefully avoid Bob for the rest of the day!

It is two weeks later. We are still getting up potatoes. I ride in the carts as Frank leads them down the rows. The picked potatoes are left along the rows at intervals, in baskets. Frank lifts the baskets by the handles and swings them up to me. I catch them with both hands and the potatoes fall into the cart at my feet.

The job has a rhythm entirely lacking in most farm work. I am so engrossed in it, and am concentrating so hard on catching the baskets at the right moment, that I don't notice my feet getting covered in potatoes.

When we reach the end of the field the cart is full. I am supposed to lead it to the grave; but I find I can't even get out. I am buried in potatoes up to my knees.

The men gather round and laugh. I struggle and pull, but I am firmly stuck. At last I manage to pull my feet out of my boots. I lead the cart to the grave bare-footed, and recover my boots when the potatoes are emptied out. But it's a long time before I recover my dignity!

We start on the second field of potatoes. This grave is made quite near the rows, so I help to pick instead of leading carts.

In the middle of the morning, I go back to the yard. I have to help the vet to give an injection to two of my cows. Rosie and Mary-Ann are being tested for tuberculosis.

I bring them into the sheds. Soon the vet arrives—a large, comfortable-looking man with three chins. He puts a ring through the cow's nose, with a rope attached. The other end of the rope is then thrown over a beam in the roof, and I hang on to it to act as a restraining influence on the cow.

Rosie gives no trouble at all. I can see by the look on Mary-Ann's face what she thinks of it. The vet says soothingly 'Steady, old girl!' I don't know if he means me or the cow. I haul hard on the rope, shut my eyes, and hope for the best. Fortunately it doesn't take long. Later, I learn that both Mary-Ann and Rosie have passed the test.

In the evenings, I burn potato tops on the fields. Just before black-out I go round stamping out all the smouldering ashes. Anyway it keeps my feet warm.

I am engaged in this when a deep voice out of the surrounding dusk says, 'Make sure you get them out!' I jump and swing round. A man holding a gun is standing a few feet away. It is some time before I recognize him as a neighbouring farmer. I had forgotten he had permission to shoot pigeons on our land!

I go on burning tops the next morning. My watch has gone wrong, so I ask Frank to call me at twelve. It seems a very long morning. I have no idea of the time, so I just carry on. At last Frank appears at the hedge. 'Ha'n't you gone to dinner yet?' he calls in simulated astonishment.

'What time is it?' I shout back.

'Quarter to one!' says Frank. 'I clean forgot all about you!'

I don't stop to dispute the point. I dash back to my billet, hoping there's some dinner left. There is. Mrs Burrows says she is pleased to see I am so enthusiastic about my work!

At last the potatoes are finished. We start to riddle them. The riddling machine is run by a motor. On the first morning, I arrive at the field to find that no one can start the thing. Bob spends some time trying, while the rest of us just stand and watch. The tips of my fingers and toes get frozen.

At last Bob sends me to fetch Mr Brook. He comes down to the field and looks at the machine. He fiddles about with it. He turns the handle. The machine splutters and starts up. Mr Brook walks away.

Bob looks first at the machine and then at the farmer's retreating figure. 'Well, I'll be buggered!' he says. We start work.

Riddling is quite an interesting job. The potatoes revolve past under my fingers. I grab the bad ones and throw them out. I concentrate hard on them, and the time soon goes. We riddle five ton that afternoon.

The next job is threshing. We spend two days at it. When I arrive on the first day, I am told to fill the bags of chaff.

Chaff rushes out of the threshing machine in a never-ending stream. As fast as I carry one bag away, another is filled. Quite often I don't get back in time, and the chute gets blocked up with chaff.

I wear an old mackintosh, boots, and an oil-silk hood. By the time I leave off, my face is black with chaff-dust. I daren't imagine what I must look like.

When I undress, I find there is chaff in all my clothes, chaff next to my skin. It is a thousand times worse than

116

hay. I feel I understand now the reason for the saying, 'You can't catch an old bird with chaff!'

Next day I ask Bob if I can go on the stack instead. He says I can. It's hard work there, but at least it's fairly clean. When I leave off, Bob asks me which I like best.

'Well, the thing I *really* like best', I tell him, 'is sliding down off the stack at the end of the day . . .'

I 2

It is October, and the men are getting up sugarbeet. They don't need me, so after milking I clean out buildings on the farm. I have to clear out one small shed at the back of the barn. As the doorway leads into the barn, I throw the dry straw and muck out of the windows on a fork. As I throw out one forkful I see Mr Brook coming across the yard— but how am I to know he is coming to speak to me? As I throw the next forkful he puts his head in the window— and the muck hits him full in the face.

He wipes the muck out of his eyes, and I stammer profuse apologies. I am not quite sure whether he does believe that I didn't do it on purpose. But he tells me that when I have finished the shed, he wants me to clear up the loft.

The floor of the loft is covered with chaff and dust. I am not supplied with a brush and dustpan, and if I sweep it out of the doorway, it will only blow back. So I sweep it all through a crack in the floor-boards, into the hay-barn below. Too late, I realize that Mr Brook has just come into the barn, and is standing directly underneath the crack!

The next day I am told to clear up leaves in the yard. A small evacuee boy watches me. For some reason he always bursts out laughing whenever he looks in my direction. His name is Jimmy, but I call him Abbie, short for Absalom, because his mother always refers to him as 'my son'. I find him a distinct hindrance to my work. He brings his toy barrow, fills it with leaves from the rubbish heap where I have dumped them, and empties them out again in the middle of the yard.

An elm tree has been blown down in one of the fields, and Bert and I are told to saw it up. All goes well until we start on the thick part of the trunk, with Bert on the other end of the two-handled saw.

I have a feeling that there is something missing. 'An adze', I tell Bert, 'I'm sure we need an adze.' I'm not sure what an adze is, but I seem to remember it is used in wood-cutting.

Half-way through the trunk, the cut closes up. The saw is stuck in and we can't get it out. Bert goes back to tell Bob about it. He returns with a curved, wedge-shaped piece of metal and a hammer. I tell Bert, 'I told you we needed an adze'. Bert looks doubtful. But at least, I find later, it's the broken blade of an adze . . .

One afternoon Mr Brook tells me to get the spade and hack up the weeds in the drive. I ask him where the spade is. He says, 'In the garage.' Then he goes off in the car.

When I go to fetch the spade, I find the garage is locked. I go to the house and ask for the key. Pamela, the maid, informs me that the key can only be used at the master's orders, and she can't give it to me. I say that in that case I can't carry out the master's orders. Pamela says she can't help it, those are her instructions. I go to find Bob.

Bob says Mr Brook lets *him* have the key—tell Pamela *he* wants it. I go back to the house.

Pamela goes to ask Mrs Brook about it. She comes back to say that the key isn't in the house—the master has it. I say, 'Where is the master?' Pamela says she doesn't know.

I return to Bob. He says he thinks the farmer is down on the lower meadow. I set off on my bicycle to find him. Half way down the drive I find my back tyre is flat, so I get off and start to pump it up. There is a hissing sound, and when I remove the connection, all the air hisses out through the valve.

I wheel my bicycle back to the farm, and set out to walk. It begins to rain.

The farmer *is* on the lower meadow, looking at the foals. I ask him again where the spade is. 'In the garage', he says, without turning round.

'Can I have the key, then?' I ask.

'It's at the house', he replies.

By now I am cold and exasperated and rained upon. I point out that I have been told at the house that (a) I couldn't have it, (b) they hadn't got it, and (c) he had it.

Mr Brook feels through all his pockets, and then says, 'Well, I haven't got it—ask my wife.'

I set off back to the farm. It is now raining hard.

Again I go to the house. I ask Pamela if I can speak to Mrs Brook, Pamela says 'She's out.'

I ask, 'Do you know where she is, or what time she'll be back?'

Pamela doesn't. I give it up in despair.

I walk back through the garden to the yard. On the way I pass the window of the front room. I glance inside—and there, sitting by the fire, is the farmer's wife.

Now hot on the scent, I return to the house. I ask Pamela, 'Are you quite *sure* she's out?' Pamela says she will see.

A few minutes later Mrs Brook herself comes to the door. I explain the situation to her. She goes back into the house. Ten minutes goes by. Then at last she returns—with the key.

In my determined pursuit I have forgotten the time. I take the key—then look at my watch. I hand the key back. 'I'm so sorry—I shan't need it now!' I tell her. I don't wait to hear what she says. It's milking time!

I have been in the Land Army now for six months, and I have my first week's holiday. Breeched and iron-shod, I walk through the streets of my home town. A card in a jeweller's window catches my eye. On it are displayed half-a-dozen Land Army badges. The card is labelled 'Latest Novelty'.

I go into the café where I had tea after I heard that my application for enrolment had been accepted. It is Saturday evening, and the café is crowded. The wireless is playing dance music, interspersed with atmospherics, and the warm air is filled with drifting smoke. I walk down the room to the nearest table, conscious of the faint swish of my corduroys, the clatter of my iron-shod heels on the wooden floor—it sounds like a cart-horse coming in.

I sit down at a table, and the waitress approaches. I order coffee.

'It'll have to be black—sorry', she says laconically. 'No milk.'

V

Doing What Comes Naturally

I have been in the Land Army for seven months when I wake up one morning with a sore throat and a headache, and find I am aching all over when I get out of bed. I get through the morning milking feeling more and more wobbly, and at breakfast time I ask Mr Brook if I can have time off to go to the doctor.

The doctor's surgery is full, and I sit for an hour looking at a magazine that grows steadily less interesting, until at last my turn comes. The doctor, a cheerful little red-faced man, takes my temperature, which is normal, looks down my throat, and says I have tonsilitis. I say I can't have, as I had my tonsils out when I was six, but he says Yes, I can, if you haven't got tonsils you get it in the glands.

He gives me a certificate for my employer and a bottle of medicine, and tells me to go home and go to bed.

I go back to my billet and tell Mrs Burrows, who is sympathetic, and agrees that if I am going to be in bed for several days it would be better if I went home. So I telephone Mr Brook and tell him I shall have to be away sick for a few days, pack what I need, and catch the bus home.

It is a cold, damp, November day, and by the time I arrive home I am feeling very shaky and am thankful to get into bed.

The next morning I wake up feeling hot and dizzy, and my mother sends for our doctor, who finds I now have a temperature of 101° and says I have 'flu and bronchitis.

He puts me on to a course of M and B tablets and says I shall have to stay in bed for a week at least.

The next few days are hazy in my memory and I am

not sure whether it is the 'flu or the M and B which is making me feel worse. I am only vaguely conscious of the passing of time and seem to spend most of my time asleep, although it seems unfair that I feel just as ill when I am asleep as I do when I am awake.

At the end of the week I am allowed to stop taking the M and B but not to get up, and it is two weeks before I am able to get out of bed, come downstairs for an hour or two, and go back to bed again.

My mother has been keeping Mr Brook informed of my progress, and in accordance with Land Army regulations he sends me my wages at the end of each week. But at the end of the third week, when I am convalescent, I get a letter saying that he has had to replace me as they cannot wait any longer for me to recover, and giving me a week's notice.

When I am on my feet again I go to the Land Army office, where I am welcomed sympathetically, and told that they will notify me as soon as they have another job available, but as it is now only a week before Christmas this will not be until some time in the New Year; and meanwhile as I lost my job through no fault of my own I shall receive 35s a week Land Army unemployment pay.

I go home and tell my parents this and they heave a resigned sigh at the prospect of having me at home again for an indefinite period, but are quite impressed by the 35s a week.

Two weeks after Christmas I have still heard nothing from the Land Army; and I receive a letter from the editor of *Animal Life*, a magazine to which I have been contributing a nature diary for the last three years, acknowledging my last manuscript and asking Would I by any chance be interested in a job as his secretary?

When I tell my parents this my mother says, 'How nice, dear', and my father picks up his pipe from the floor and says, If I calm down a bit perhaps he will be able to understand what I am talking about.

When I have calmed down I show them the editor's

letter and my father says That's all very well, but he thought I was in the Land Army.

I say Surely I can resign from the Land Army? and my father says he thinks it would be a pity, and my mother says Now I am registered for National Service will the Labour Exchange allow me to take a civilian job?

I say '—— the Labour Exchange!' and my mother says I ought not to use that kind of language, and I say I learned it in the Land Army.

My father heaves a sigh and picks up the morning paper, saying that I'd better go to the Labour Exchange and see what they say.

I retire to my room and write to Simon P. Shaw, the editor, saying that I would very much like the job if the authorities will allow me to take it, and asking him to write me a formal letter offering me the position so that I can show it at the Labour Exchange.

Within a few days I receive his reply, and armed with this I go to the Labour Exchange. Here I am interviewed by a woman with glasses and auburn hair, who reads the letter and informs me coldly that there is no chance at all of my being allowed to take the job, and if I resign from the Land Army I shall be directed into some other form of War Work immediately.

I leave disheartened, and call at the Land Army office on the way home, where I am informed that they haven't got any news of a job for me, but will Let me know.

When I get home and tell my parents this my mother says it is too bad of the Land Army to keep me hanging about like this, and I point out that so far as I can see I would be more usefully employed as an editor's secretary than in being kept waiting about at the Government's expense.

My father unexpectedly says He supposes I could resign from the Land Army and take the job and see what happens, and my mother says Why not go and see Simon P. Shaw and see what he thinks?

So the next morning I telephone Mr Shaw and suggest

that I should come up to London to see him, and he is most charming and says he would like to see me too; and I arrange to go for an interview on the following Wednesday afternoon.

On Wednesday morning I catch the early train to London. On arriving at Liverpool Street I walk up the platform and am immediately enveloped in a dense cloud of hot black smoke, which makes me feel as if I had entered Hell and was about to come before judgment; but what I actually come before after emerging at the other side of it is the wrong underground train. I do not discover this until I am on it, so then I get out and return to Liverpool Street. This time I find the right train and eventually arrive at Waterloo, which appears to me about the size of a small village, and where I eventually find the right platform and catch a train to Richmond, where *Animal Life* has temporary offices due to the War.

Coming out of Richmond station I follow the instructions given me by Mr Shaw and find the *Animal Life* offices, which are, most appropriately, in a room that used to be a hay-loft, over the stable which had been converted into a garage and is now used by Simon P. Shaw as the magazine's printing works.

I knock at the front door of the house where there is a plate with the name of the magazine on it, and after a long wait I am admitted by one of the printing staff—or rather, as I learn later, by *the* printing staff—whose name is Harry. He takes me down a passage at the far end of the hall which leads into the workshop, and there I find Simon P. Shaw, wrapped up in an overcoat, sitting on a pile of magazines correcting proof sheets for the next issue.

He explains that he has 'flu but he didn't want to ask me to postpone my interview, and I tell him that he ought to be in bed. Only afterwards it occurs to me that this is rather an odd remark with which to open an interview with a prospective employer.

Simon P. Shaw is tall and thin, with fluffy brown hair and a small brown moustache, and for some reason looks exactly like a squirrel. I am so struck by this resemblance that when he stands up I find myself looking to see whether he has a large fluffy tail behind.

He takes me upstairs to the office in the hay-loft and I explain to him the position about the Labour Exchange, and he says he is quite willing to take me on without their permission, and try to get them to agree to my staying with him after that. He explains that he is at present trying to produce the magazine almost single-handed, except for Harry who isn't really a printer at all but a builder's labourer, and he urgently needs someone to handle the secretarial work.

I tell him I think I could do this and that I would like the job very much, and he says that my position will be that of assistant editor, and I can start as soon as I like at a salary of £4 a week.

I say that I will start as soon as I can find rooms in Richmond, and he says he will try to find somewhere for me, and will let me know as soon as he has; and I leave the office walking on air.

Fortunately I remember to walk on the air that leads back to Richmond station, and after getting lost again at Waterloo, I eventually find my way to Liverpool Street and catch my train home.

The train is held up by four air raid warnings on the way but I reach home at last, and inform my parents that I am now an Assistant Editor.

2

The next day I write to the Land Army stating that I wish to resign and take up some other work which does not involve my being 'stood off' for long indefinite periods. Within a week I receive a letter telling me that my resignation has been accepted, and they have notified the Labour

Exchange that I am now available for another job. The same day I receive a telephone call from Simon P. Shaw.

He says that he has not been able to find rooms for me but he wants me to start work straight away. Can I come up in two days' time if he books a room for me temporarily at a private hotel? I say that I can, and after informing my mother of the latest move, I write to Mr Shaw confirming that I will arrive on the following Thursday.

The next morning I receive a letter from Mr Shaw saying that he has booked a room for me at the Avonmore Hotel, and I can stay there while I am finding myself permanent accommodation; and he is looking forward to my joining him on the following day.

Now that it is all settled my father looks stern and says he hopes that I have done the right thing, and my mother says that Richmond seems a terribly long way away but Mr Shaw had a very nice voice when she spoke to him on the telephone.

I dare not tell her that I think I am starting a sore throat, so I say that if I had stayed in the Land Army I might have been sent to Scotland and I am much more likely to make a career in publishing than on the land, and then I finish my packing and go to bed.

The next morning when I wake up I have a very painful sore throat and find difficulty in eating my breakfast, but my parents put this down to excitement and don't ask questions.

I catch my train for Liverpool Street after saying goodbye to my mother at the gate and my father at the station, and try to concentrate on being an assistant editor, but am increasingly conscious only of the pain in my throat. By the time I reach London I am feeling very hot and my head aches, and I think that when I get to the hotel I had better telephone Mr Shaw and go to bed.

I find my way to Richmond and, after a number of enquiries, to the Avonmore Hotel, where I ask about my room. The reception clerk goes away for some time and then comes back to say that they cannot find any trace of a room booked in my name. I explain that it was booked for me by Mr Shaw of *Animal Life*, and the clerk goes away again and then comes back and says Yes, they have a room booked for a Mrs Shaw.

By this time I am feeling too ill to sort this out, let alone consider all the possible implications, and it is obvious to me that I am in no condition to deal with it now, or to start a new job. I reluctantly decide it would be better to make a fresh start on a more satisfactory basis, and I leave the hotel and return to Waterloo.

It is six o'clock by the time I reach Liverpool Street, but owing to air raids all the trains are running late. I catch the 5.46 train which actually leaves at 9 o'clock, and then stops for over an hour with all the lights out before it has gone half-way.

As it is a slow train anyway it is midnight when it gets in, and I am feeling half dead by the time I get home. My parents are in bed and asleep and the house is locked up, so I have to announce my arrival by throwing handfuls of gravel at their bedroom window, much to the annoyance of my father who wakes under the impression that it is machine-gun fire. But anyway he lets me in, and after a brief explanation my mother gets me a hot drink and some aspirin and I go to bed.

I am in bed for two days with laryngitis, and my mother telephones Simon P. Shaw and explains why I did not arrive at the office. I do not tell her that the room at the hotel had been booked for a Mrs Shaw, because I feel that if I do I shall probably not be allowed to return to Richmond at all.

On the third day I get up and after making a number of enquiries by telephoning various social welfare organizations in Richmond, I eventually succeed in obtaining temporary accommodation at a girls' hostel. I also telephone Mr Shaw and tell him this, and he apologizes profusely for the muddle over the booking at the hotel.

Three days later, a week after my first abortive attempt, I set off again for Waterloo.

3

This time I complete my journey to Richmond via Waterloo uneventfully, and after many enquiries locate the Girls' Hostel which is situated, improbably, in Paradise Road; and am met by the Superintendent, whose name, even more improbably, is Miss Sweeting.

Miss Sweeting is a grey-haired elderly woman who greets me with the information that she is suffering from a strained back as a result of falling off a table after talking to me on the telephone. I am puzzled as to whether it is her normal practice to take telephone calls on the table but she does not enlighten me about this.

However, she shows me my room, which to my relief is a single bedroom at the top of the house, as I had been rather afraid that I was going to share a dormitory.

When I have unpacked some of my things I go out and call at the *Animal Life* offices and let Mr Shaw know that I have arrived this time and that I will start work at 9.30 on the following day. Then I return to the hostel for tea, which consists of cold rice pudding in the kitchen; and I am introduced by Miss Sweeting to the other residents of the hostel.

These are Betty, a tall fair girl of sixteen who, Miss Sweeting tells me, has been sent here for six months to get her away from bad influences in her home; Noreen, who is eighteen, and according to Miss Sweeting was married at sixteen, had a baby, left her husband and took up with a Newfoundland soldier who had deserted from the Army, provided him with civilian clothes, and was sent here by her Probation Officer after serving a sentence in Holloway prison; and Gwen, a cousin of Noreen's, short, fat, and seventeen, who, Miss Sweeting says, had an illegitimate child still-born two years ago and has been sent here to keep her from the advances of her immoral father.

When I have taken all this in I feel somewhat stunned, and it is apparent to me that I have landed myself in a

Home for Difficult Girls and not as I had previously supposed a hostel for girls in difficulties. I realize that I am quite out of place here having nothing more spectacular on my record than evading the Labour Exchange to become an assistant editor.

The next morning I get up and come down for breakfast, consisting of lumpy porridge, weak tea, and bread and margarine, which we get for ourselves as Miss Sweeting has breakfast in bed. Noreen says morosely that the food is better in Holloway as they have brown sugar and she used to eat it on her bread and margarine; and from this rather depressing background I set out to start my first day's work.

When I arrive at the office Mr Shaw shows me the typewriter and hands me a pile of correspondence to deal with, and goes away to the workshop to set up type.

I stare at the pile of letters with something approaching terror, but eventually I sort them out into subscriptions, requests for specimen copies of the magazine, and other letters, and by the time I have dealt with the subscriptions and specimen copies it is time for lunch.

After lunch I tackle the letters and succeed in dealing with most of them although it is difficult to answer an enquiry about a missing number on a subscription which you cannot trace, from a reader whose name you can't decipher, and whose letter is dated three months previously anyway.

So I adopt the system of sending the required number of the magazine to anyone who complains they haven't had one, writing asking for further details to those that I can't trace, and sending letters of apology to all those dated more than two weeks previously, explaining that the magazine has been seriously understaffed and that their query is being dealt with.

This takes all the rest of the day and by the evening I am still left with a pile of letters either requiring further investigation or awaiting further information, and a pile of letters in reply which I place on Mr Shaw's desk, feeling somewhat apprehensive and totally exhausted. But Mr Shaw comes up from the workshop and signs all the letters I have typed without comment, so I revive and go out to find a café where I can have a proper tea.

On the way I see in a newsagent's window a card advertising a Bed-sitting-room To Let, at 27s 6d a week, breakfast and Sunday dinner included; so I call and make enquiries about it.

The landlady is a little dark Cornish woman who takes me up to the top of the house and shows me a tiny attic room with a little window tucked in under the roof looking over Richmond Green, with a divan bed and a table and a chair and an electric radiator, and practically nothing else. But it is clean and quiet and I am not enthusiastic about staying any longer at the hostel, so I arrange to take it and move in when it is free, at the end of the week.

Then I return to the hostel and have supper of baked beans and cocoa, with Miss Sweeting and Betty and Gwen in the kitchen. At about nine o'clock Betty and Gwen go upstairs, and Miss Sweeting talks to me at great length and in great detail about all the girls' pasts, which makes me think longingly about my bed-sitting-room.

At ten o'clock Noreen comes in slightly drunk, and while Miss Sweeting is dealing with this I go to bed.

4

When I arrive at the office to start my second day's work I am no longer apprehensive, and feel very conscious of being an assistant editor. I am dealing with the morning's post when Mr Shaw comes up from the workshop and hands me a pile of printed post-cards informing subscribers that their subscriptions are due for renewal, and asks me to address them as quickly as possible to the people whose subscriptions have expired. I spend the rest of the day doing this, and take them to the post when I leave off at 5.30.

When I get back to the hostel I find Noreen sitting in the kitchen in tears, because, she says, she wants to go home to see her baby the next day, and Miss Sweeting won't let her go. This depresses me horribly, as although I am not altogether sure it is her baby she wants to see, she is obviously very unhappy.

The next morning when I come down to breakfast—which is cornflakes, without milk or sugar—I find the three girls in a state of unrest. Whispering and nudges between them indicate that something out of the ordinary is going on, and eventually Noreen confides to me that she is going to run away. The others are apparently undecided whether to go with her or not. I don't feel that I can do anything to prevent this, and I am sure that if I had to live here permanently, I would run away myself; so I agree not to tell Miss Sweeting and leave for the office.

I spend all day sorting out and dealing with more long-overdue letters, and when I return to the hostel in the evening I find the atmosphere stormy—all three girls have run away, and Miss Sweeting is in a furious temper. As I come in she is putting on her coat and hat, and she informs me that if I want any tea I can have some bread and cheese when she comes back, and she goes out and slams the door. So I also go out, shutting the door quietly, and have tea again at a café in the town.

The next evening when I come in, after spending most of the day checking manuscripts and doing some book reviews for the next issue of the magazine, I find Noreen has come back, and Miss Sweeting is questioning her with a view to locating and rounding up the others.

According to Noreen she and the other two had been to Cardiff with three soldiers, came back the next morning, and have spent the rest of the time in pubs round Victoria. Questioned further, she says that she thinks Gwen went off with a Canadian soldier and might now be in Scotland, and when she last saw Betty she was planning to go to

Cornwall in the company of a short dark man in civilian clothes with a small moustache.

Miss Sweeting asks sharply, 'Who was he?' and struck by the inanity of the question in the circumstances I say, 'Hitler, obviously' and Miss Sweeting is not amused.

It seems to me that Miss Sweeting is not really very interested in the recovery of the missing girls and is inclined to dwell too lingeringly on the less savoury aspect of their activities. She agrees however when Noreen suggests that she should go back and try to find them, but refuses to give her the money for the fare. I feel that this is an unwise move as if Noreen has her fare paid by someone on the way it seems unlikely that she will end up where she is intended to, so I offer to finance the expedition to the extent of half-a-crown, and Noreen accepts this and departs, presumably for Victoria.

Miss Sweeting predicts, without apparent distress, that she will not come back again, and proceeds to describe with positive relish how she envisages Noreen will in fact be occupied. I endure this because the kitchen where Miss Sweeting is sitting is the only warm room in the house; and at ten o'clock Noreen returns, alone, but saying that she has seen Gwen and thinks she will come back the next day.

In the morning Noreen is sent home by Miss Sweeting, who says she refuses to keep her any longer. That night shortly before ten o'clock Gwen returns, and says that she has been with an American soldier who wants to marry her as soon as he can get permission to do so.

Miss Sweeting snorts and says, 'A likely story', and tells her to go to bed, which although an eminently suitable exhortation, does seem, coming at this point in the conversation, a little unfortunate.

Anyway Gwen does as she is told, and Miss Sweeting settles down in her chair and starts telling me about the man she was engaged to when she was a girl, who was killed in the last war.

'There was no silly sentiment about it', she says smugly, 'we just liked each other and I knew we would be happy married'—but by now I have had enough of the oddities of human behaviour, so I also go to bed.

The next day is Saturday and I have the afternoon free, but I feel that all Sunday at the hostel with Miss Sweeting will be more than I can stand, and as Mr Shaw has told me he usually goes on working at the office on Sundays, I ask him if I can come in and help, and he says Yes, certainly I can if I want to.

On Saturday afternoon I do some shopping and get ready to move into my bed-sitting-room; and I spend Sunday typing out articles on the oddities of animal behaviour, which I find extremely refreshing.

In the evening I go back to the hostel for the last time, and am informed by Miss Sweeting that Betty has returned; but I escape to my room before she can go into details, finish packing my things, and finally say goodbye to Miss Sweeting, who is then in her sitting-room playing 'For he's a jolly good fellow', over and over with two fingers on the piano.

I am welcomed by my new landlady, whose name is Miss Kneebone, and install myself in my attic room, which Miss Kneebone describes cheerfully as 'the nearest you can get to heaven!' After my week at the hostel, it really does seem like paradise.

5

After I have settled into my bed-sitting-room, looking back on my first week in Richmond is rather like remembering a nightmare; the only waking intervals being my hours at the office. I unpack my typewriter, an ancient and somewhat unwieldy machine which used to be in my father's office, and spend my evenings typing a cat story I have written as a serial for *Animal Life*.

One Monday morning Mr Shaw comes over to my desk and shows me a letter he has just received from a Dr Mary

Brown, who runs an Animal Shelter on the other side of London. We are going to publish an account of her work in the magazine—and Simon P. wants me to go and see the shelter, and interview the doctor, and write a story about it. He seems to assume that I can do this as a matter of course, and I try to look as if I can, although I am not at all certain as I have never interviewed anyone before.

'She says she wants us to come on a Tuesday afternoon,' Mr Shaw adds, 'as "all the little—somethings—come in for their operations then"—I can't read her writing', he explains, frowning over the letter. 'I can't make this word out—probably it's "dears".'

I agree that this is probable, but I cannot read the word either.

'So you'd better go tomorrow', resumes Mr Shaw, and he gives me directions about crossing London.

The next day I set off, and eventually arrive at the Animal Shelter, and meet Dr Brown. She is a grey-haired but middle-aged lady with a rather vague face. We sit down in her office and I do my best to extract from her not only the factual details about the daily work of the shelter, but any more enlivening incidents that will interest our readers; but I find that either I am no good at interviewing, or Dr Brown is an exceptionally difficult person from whom to extract information.

It does appear that the main function of the shelter is to chloroform sick and unwanted animals, but I feel that constant repetition of this is not what Simon P. sent me here for. In reply to my repeated enquiries Dr Brown says No, she doesn't think there have been any unusual incidents or animals that she can tell me about; and it is only after much further probing that she remembers a fox, found running about the streets of London, which was brought to the Shelter—and immediately chloroformed.

Depressed by this, I am relieved when it is time for Dr Brown to take me into the surgery to watch the 'operations'. But my relief is rapidly replaced by horror when I realize that the 'operations' consist entirely of the neutering of young male cats. I firmly believe that our creation is better left as the Creator designed it; and that the purpose of all life is the procreation of its children. It seems to me it is better to kill any creature, than to take its life—and not let it die.

I do not say this, however, but I cannot meet the cats' eyes as they go under the anaesthetic, and I am thankful when it is all over and I can get away.

When I get back to the office Mr Shaw asks me how I got on and I tell him that I seem to have spent the day in a lethal chamber, and Mr Shaw nods sympathetically and says he was afraid it might be like that. He adds, 'What about the operations?' and I tell him briefly and pointedly, 'The word we couldn't read was "toms".'

Mr Shaw looks startled and says, 'Do you mean you had to spend the whole afternoon watching *that*?' and I say I did, and I don't agree with the neutering of cats.

Simon P. says he doesn't either; and then we get on with the rest of the day's work.

About a week after this Mr Shaw tells me I am to go to Gloucester and get a story about guard dogs. Apparently a Colonel Baxter is in charge of training dogs for guard duties there, and Simon P. has arranged for me to be shown over the training camp.

Early the next morning I set off by train for Gloucester. Mr Shaw has told me that there will be someone at the station to take me to the camp, but I am staggered when I am met on the platform by the Colonel himself. He escorts me to a waiting car and takes me to a restaurant for lunch. Here I start asking for background information, having no idea of how to make social conversation with a Colonel anyway, but am hampered, in addition to my growing nervousness, by the difficulty of asking questions while consuming alphabet soup.

I am relieved when the meal is over, and we set off for the training camp. Here I walk round the kennels, watch the dogs at work, and am introduced to their handlers; still escorted by the Colonel, who seems reluctant to leave my side. He also seems to be suffering from nervousness, and as time goes on looks repeatedly at his watch. Finally when I have seen everything I can, I ask him if he has any photographs of the dogs at work which we could use, and he says he has some at his home, and will take me to look at them before I go.

As we drive to his house the Colonel explains that his wife is out and will not be back until late in the evening; and I also gather that his superior officers do not altogether approve of his dogs receiving publicity, and the Colonel is anxious that I should not be seen near the camp by anyone else in authority.

When we arrive the Colonel takes me into his drawing-room, and shows me a collection of photographs of the dogs, from which I pick out half-a-dozen which I think will appeal to Mr Shaw. The Colonel goes on looking at the clock, and says if he drives me straight to the station I can catch the 3.15 train. So we go back to the car and he drives at great speed to the station.

Unfortunately we are held up at two traffic lights, and reach the station three minutes after the train has left. I say it doesn't matter, as I can easily wait at the station for the next one; but the Colonel doesn't appear happy about this, and says if he drives very fast to the next station, he can get me there in time to catch the train.

So we get into the car again and the Colonel drives very fast and we pull into the station yard as the train draws up at the platform. But the platform is on the other side of the station, separated from the yard by a high iron fence with spikes on top; and the only way to get to the train is by going out of the yard, round by the road, and over the bridge, by which time the train will have gone.

I still cannot see why I could not wait for the next train, but by now the Colonel appears to regard my departure on this one as a matter of vital military importance.

'You can catch it if you climb over the fence', he says. 'Come on—I'll help you over!'

I am used to climbing fences, but not with the help of

Colonels, and not in my best clothes. I take hold of the rails and scramble up, with the Colonel pushing me from behind.

Several people in the train are looking out of the windows at us, obviously wondering what is going on.

I pull myself up to the top, balancing precariously on the top rail with the Colonel still supporting me in the rear, and swing my legs over. The Colonel lets go, and I jump down on the other side.

By now quite a number of people in the train are watching with great interest.

I say 'Goodbye' to the Colonel with all the dignity I can manage, run across the line and tear up the platform, and just as the train starts, jump into the nearest carriage door.

Out of the opposite window I see the Colonel waving enthusiastically. I lean out of the window and wave back. I cannot help feeling that I might have departed more unobtrusively, if that is what he wanted, if I had waited for the next train.

I walk through the crowded carriages looking for a seat. All the other passengers stare at me as I pass, with expressions ranging from shocked disapproval to frankly suggestive grins.

When at last I find a seat I get out my notes and start to write my story. An explanation occurs to me as I describe how the dogs are trained to guard places of importance and tackle anyone who has to be kept away. Obviously the Colonel is such an enthusiast in his work that he has given me a personal demonstration of a guard dog in action.

6

I have been working on *Animal Life* for a month, and I am beginning to think that the Government has forgotten about me, when I receive a peremptory letter telling me to call at once at the Labour Exchange.

When I go to the Labour Exchange I am interviewed by a girl of about my own age who tells me I cannot go on working for *Animal Life* and I shall be directed into some form of War Work immediately.

I go back to the office and tell Mr Shaw this, and he says he will write to the Labour Exchange asking for me to be allowed to continue in my present employment.

Shortly after this I have an encounter with my landlady who says that the other residents are complaining about the noise of my typewriter in the evenings. Apparently being at the top of the house it makes the whole building vibrate, and gives everyone else the impression that there is an air raid in progress.

I say I am sorry but I do not see what I can do about it, so the next morning I go round to the newsagents where I saw my room advertised, to see if there is any other room to let. I am rather taken aback to find what is unmistakably my present room being advertised to let again, and when I ask in the shop for the address I find I am right.

There is also another bed-sitting-room advertised, so I get the address of this too, and go to see it. This house is only a few hundred yards further down Richmond Green, and the landlady, a cheerful middle-aged woman in glasses, shows me a large front room on the ground floor with a bed, table and chairs, wardrobe, dressing-table, and a big settee in front of an open fireplace. Compared with my present room it is luxury, and Mrs Goodman, the landlady, says that she doesn't object to a typewriter at all, so long as I don't bring in Men. I say that I only have a typewriter, and I arrange to move in at the end of the week.

Then I go back and give notice to Miss Kneebone, explaining that as I see she is already advertising my room I feel she will probably find it more convenient to have it vacant. Miss Kneebone vehemently denies this, but I say that in any case I have found other accommodation where there is no objection to my typewriter, and she goes out and slams the door. A week later I move into my new home.

By this time Mr Shaw has received a reply to his letter from the Labour Exchange, saying that under no circumstances can I be permitted to remain in his employment and I will be directed into War Work forthwith.

I say I am quite willing to carry on with him until I am removed by force, and Simon P. says he doesn't know whether they would go as far as that but anyway he wants to keep me as long as he can.

We are now in the middle of sending out the current issue of the magazine, and as this involves addressing several hundred envelopes as quickly as possible, I suggest that I should come back in the evening to get them done.

Although it is only February there is a softness now in the air, which I feel is probably the nearest Richmond can get to the awakening of an early spring. When I go out for tea I pass a pair of ragged gypsy children on the pavement selling willow baskets of moss and primroses. I buy one, and take it back with me to the office.

When we have finished addressing the envelopes and putting the magazines into them, we have to check the addresses back on the card index to make sure that none have been missed. Mr Shaw says Would I like to go now? but I say If it will help I would rather stay and finish checking the envelopes.

I sit by Mr Shaw's desk with a pile of envelopes on my lap, watching him as he works through the card index, and a scented silence drifts in through the open window, reminding me again of Spring.

When I get back to my room I put my primroses in the middle of the table, and lie in bed looking at them until I fall asleep.

A few days later I am typing letters and Mr Shaw is working at his desk when he suddenly looks up and says, Would I care to go to the theatre with him on Saturday?

I hear myself say that I would, thank you, and then Mr Shaw gets up and goes down to the printing works.

I go on sitting in front of the typewriter, and after some time it occurs to me that he will know from the silence that I am not typing, so I get on with the letters again, but somehow I find it very difficult to concentrate on my work.

On Saturday afternoon I meet Mr Shaw at the office, and we walk across the Green to the theatre. I do not notice very much about the play, but afterwards we go to a café for tea; and during tea we talk about *Animal Life*, and my nature diary.

Mr Shaw tells me that he was called up for the Army, through a mistake, early in the War, and he had pneumonia and spent several months in hospital before being discharged. He says he has been interested in me ever since I first started writing for the magazine; and I tell him that I cannot keep up my diary now I am not living in the country, but I have just finished writing a cat story which he might be able to use in its place, and he says he would like to see it, and tells me about his dog that he had for eight years, which died a few days before I came to Richmond.

He asks if I like being in Richmond, and I say I do, but I get homesick for the country; and he says, Would I come for a walk with him on Sunday, and see the countryside beyond the town?

After tea we walk back to my room together, and Mr Shaw says Goodnight to me on my doorstep, and I go in feeling rather dazed and with my head full of stars. I sing all the while I am undressing and getting ready for bed, until I have to stop because I find that it is not possible to sing and wash my face at the same time.

On Sunday afternoon Mr Shaw calls for me at my room, and we take a bus out of Richmond and walk through some rather stilted sort of woods, and see some surprisingly artificial-looking cows coming in to be milked at a rather dusty-looking farm. We take the ferry across the river, and when we get back to Richmond I ask Mr Shaw into my room for a cup of tea.

I light my fire and boil the kettle on the hearth, and we

sit on the settee and watch the dancing flames making patterns in the fire.

'I'm glad you came to work with me', Mr Shaw says, still looking into the fire. 'I've been very lonely since my dog died . . .'

Hesitantly I say, 'Perhaps I could take his place . . .'

Then Simon Shaw puts his hand over mine, and I am conscious of a paralysing shyness, so that I am afraid to move my hand in case he thinks I am pulling it away, but cannot think of any way to show him what I feel.

After a little while he moves his hand and take me in his arms. He kisses me gently, and I find that I am no longer paralysed, and I know now what to do next.

After quite a long time Simon sighs and says, 'I never intended to get married . . .' Then he addeds, 'You will marry me—won't you?'

I say contentedly, 'I'll marry you tomorrow, if you like.'

After another long time Simon says, 'Will you mind living in a town?'

'I wouldn't mind living anywhere with you', I tell him dreamily, 'but I'd like to bring up our babies in the country.'

Simon smiles at me. 'Do you want to have babies?' he says.

'Yes', I say firmly. 'As many as I can.'